Discard

Ripple Effects

Ten West Michigan Nonprofits Serve, Inspire, Transform

"Each time a man stands up for an ideal, or acts to improve the lot of others, or strikes out against injustice, he sends forth a tiny ripple of hope, and those ripples build a current which can sweep down the mightiest walls of oppression and resistance."
–Robert F. Kennedy

Table of Contents

Foreword

As dedicated and experienced personal historians, Betty Epperly and Deb Moore have written poignant and insightful stories focusing on the ways key West Michigan nonprofit organizations have transformed the lives of countless residents. The profiles demonstrate the significance of the nonprofits to the well being of the community, and the reader comes away better informed of the importance and impact these groups have on individuals and families. The stories in this anthology shine a light on critical concerns such as the alleviation of poverty, the assurance of proper medical treatment and food security, the importance of education and the promotion of home ownership to build a robust economy.

The Greater Grand Rapids nonprofit sector is well known throughout the state and indeed the country for its vibrancy and diversity. There is an attitude, an expectation and a desire that we roll up our sleeves and address complex issues. Our interconnected philanthropic community—comprised of individuals, foundations, corporations, faith-based organizations and nonprofits—understands the importance of collaboration. There is tremendous respect and confidence in our nonprofits; they set an example of service that encourages others to engage and give back.

Read these profiles and be inspired to get involved!

Diana R. Sieger
President
Grand Rapids Community Foundation

Preface

Ripple Effects began as a conversation between two personal historians motivated by the power of stories. While brainstorming and researching subject matter for a joint writing project, we were impressed by the abundance of agencies in Grand Rapids and West Michigan available to help people in their times of need. From that discussion we homed in on telling the stories of ten nonprofits with local roots, including five stories from each that would exemplify how the organization makes a critical difference in the lives of those they **serve**. Along the way we've been **inspired** by the staff, volunteers and clients of the agencies and the resources we've discovered in our community. As we moved forward we discovered ripple effects everywhere we looked; when people's lives are **transformed**, so often they are motivated to pay it forward.

We thank the leaders and boards of each nonprofit for their participation and many efforts in the completion this anthology. They include Sam Beals and Connie Frazier of Wedgwood Christian Services; Dave Jacobs of Home Repair Services; Mary K. Hoodhood and Christine Lentine of Kids' Food Basket; Bruce Roller and Shawn Keener of United Church Outreach Ministry; Mark Thomson and Katy Buck of D.A. Blodgett-St. John's; Melissa Werkman of Down Syndrome Association of West Michigan; Paula Veneklase and Sandy Lowery of HELP Pregnancy Crisis Aid; Melanie Beelen of Baxter Community Center; Karen Kaashoek and Ron Rozema of Catherine's Health Center; and Cheryl Schuch of Family Promise of Grand Rapids. We also thank the people who allowed us to share their stories. It was a privilege to listen to voices that we rarely hear. We hope that by reading these stories you will be inspired to support the many transforming nonprofits in the area.

Deb Moore
Betty Epperly
Grand Rapids, Michigan
October 2014

WEDGWOOD
CHRISTIAN SERVICES

TRANSFORMING LIVES ONE **CHILD** AT A TIME

Mission: *Extending God's love to youth and families through professional counseling and educational services*

"Communion" sculpture in front of Wedgwood's Nagel Chapel

3300 36th Street SE
Grand Rapids, MI 49512
616.942.2110
wedgwood.org

– Wedgwood Christian Services –

Roots

In the late 1950s Jean Boelkins and Dorothy Huizinga had concerns about the juvenile court system in Grand Rapids. They asked Rev. Jacob Eppinga of LaGrave Christian Reformed Church to tour the juvenile court facility since he could do so as a pastor, and his report confirmed miserable conditions. At the same time Harvey VanderArk was inspired by a story in the *Saturday Evening Post* about a man who founded a home for troubled and homeless boys.

As neglected children's needs became known in the Grand Rapids community, Boelkins, Huizinga and VanderArk, as well as individuals from various congregations and denominations, purchased a home in 1960 where young boys could stay with house parents and receive counseling. This home, located on the estate of Dr. Llewellyn Wedgwood in Wyoming, was once a stop on the Underground Railroad. Tunnels extended from the home's basement to nearby Buck Creek to permit easy escape by runaway slaves.

Wedgwood Acres Christian Home For Boys, 1960

At the same time a group of concerned citizens who volunteered at a citywide Youth For Christ rally became aware of the plight of neglected, directionless young people in the community. Many teens came forward at the rally and expressed emotional and spiritual needs. A steering committee that met at the home of Dr. and Mrs. Donald Johns became further sensitized to the needs of young people and found that teenage girls were underserved. In an effort to meet the needs of this marginalized segment of the population, Christian Youth Homes was incorporated in 1960. Calvary's Dr. Paul Louis Lehman and congregants from Calvary and other congregations and denominations led this new organization. In 1961 a girls' home was opened at 333 Fountain Street.

Growing Needs Lead to Combined Forces

Wedgwood Acres Christian Home for Boys opened Brookside Home in 1967, and Christian Youth Homes opened a second girls' home in 1969 on Lake Drive. The two organizations combined in 1970, and Wedgwood Acres-Christian Youth Homes was formed. A "whole person" philosophy of treatment had already emerged: one that encompassed the emotional, physical, social, intellectual and spiritual needs of the client.

Residential homes filled a gap in the Grand Rapids community, yet referrals were turned away almost daily due to lack of space. Two additional residential homes were built in the '70s, as well as new Kentwood campus offices and the *Huizinga Administration Building and Counseling Center.*

In the 1980s *Residential Treatment Centers* expanded and the *Employment Training Program* opened in Wyoming to assist teens in developing life skills. Christ and His message of hope, healing and wholeness were offered to children through the *Chaplaincy Program* and the *Wedgwood Christian Counseling Center,* both opened in 1989. The *Wedgwood Foundation* began in 1990 as an auxiliary entity with the purpose of building assets for the future benefit of the organization.

Demand for residential services continued to exceed supply. Honey Creek Homes merged with Wedgwood to provide foster care in the 1990s, and an *Independent Living* program was developed. Spiritual life flourished through the *Chaplaincy* and *Young Life* programs in the new *Nagel Chapel and Conference Center.*

A Full Continuum of Care

In 2002 the organization was renamed Wedgwood Christian Services to reflect the full continuum of care. This decade brought significant developments in the field of education with the advent of *Lighthouse Academy* (now a charter school) and *Wedgwood Institute.* To meet ongoing needs, the *Substance Abuse Outreach Services, Community-Based Prevention Services* and *Home Based Family Counseling Services* began.

Since 2010 Wedgwood has continued to expand professional counseling services. The *Parramore and VanderArk Homes* were designated recently to serve children with developmental disabilities, and *Hope Academy of West Michigan* was opened in 2011. Wedgwood's *Manasseh Project Trauma Recovery Center* opened in October 2012 to offer safety and compassion to girls who have been the victims of sex trafficking.

Programs and Services

Sam Beals, Wedgwood President and CEO, notes that by the time children arrive at the agency they have often experienced multiple traumas, innumerable losses and the sense that their lives have no meaning. Wedgwood's staff strives continually to offer grace, promote healing and encourage learning. Wedgwood's *Core Services (Community, Education and*

10

Residential) are fully funded by financial support through public sources, and *Transforming Services* are funded 100% through donor contributions.

Community Services: A broad range of quality treatment services can be utilized by anyone in the West Michigan community.

- *The Autism Center for Child Development* provides early intensive behavioral intervention for young children on the autism spectrum.
- *Professional Counseling Services* offers various types of treatment for family members with life changes or mental health concerns.
- *Substance Abuse Treatment* offers prevention and intensive treatment services to help individuals overcome alcohol and drug addiction.
- *Community Outreach* establishes after-school programs and youth groups that encourage healthy behaviors through fun activities in a safe and caring environment.
- *Prevention Services* increase resiliency against pregnancies, sexually transmitted diseases, substance use, violence and other high-risk behaviors among teenagers.
- *Home Based Counseling Services* target prevention of abuse, neglect and out-of-home placement through counseling for children and families undergoing relational, emotional and substance abuse crises.

Education Services: *Lighthouse Academy*, launched in 2005, has operated as a charter school under Ferris State University since 2008. The school provides students who are expelled, adjudicated, or placed according to an Individualized Education Program a crucial opportunity to complete their education. In 2012 a North Campus was established to serve the same student  population. *Lighthouse Academy* provides educational services to students at Wedgwood Christian Services, D.A. Blodgett-St. Johns, the Kent County Juvenile Detention Center (the Waalkes School) and The Haven.

Hope Academy of West Michigan, a charter school since 2011 serving preschool–12th grade students in the Garfield Park/Burton Heights neighborhoods of inner-city Grand Rapids, offers at-risk students renewed hope for academic success through a holistic teaching approach.

The *Wedgwood Institute* offers diverse continuing education to employees and community professionals who work with children. These programs strengthen the quality of care for troubled youth and families.

Residential Services: Wedgwood's 11 residential programs include 24-hour care and individualized professional treatment for children and adolescents within a caring, Christian environment. Services include individual, family and group therapy, specialized education services and medical services.

- *Abuse, Neglect, Delinquency, Mental Health:* Wedgwood offers secure treatment for male and female youth between the ages of 8-17 who have experienced abuse and neglect, who are in the juvenile delinquency system, or who have significant mental health concerns.
- *Autistic/Developmentally Disabled:* Wedgwood's Developmental Treatment Specialists assist children with developmental disabilities to maximize potential so they can return to less restrictive settings.

- *Sexual Offending Behavior:* Intensive treatment is available for adolescent males ages 10-17. Professionally trained staff provide close supervision and milieu therapy. A specialized unit provides care for boys who are lower functioning.
- *Respite Care* and *Crisis Care* is available for youth ages 6-17 to meet the needs of children with mental health issues and their families who need a therapeutic break or crisis intervention.
- *Sex Trafficking:* As part of Wedgwood's *Manasseh Project*, a trauma recovery center provides shelter and a trauma-focused treatment program for girls who are the victims of sex trafficking and other forms of severe sexual abuse.
- *Short Term Group Home:* Short-term intensive treatment is provided to boys and girls ages 6-17.
- *Substance Abuse:* This program is available for adolescents ages 12-17 who abuse substances and may have a co-occurring mental health diagnosis.

Transforming Services: As one of Michigan's most regarded experts for helping hurting youth and families since 1960, Wedgwood Christian Services is dedicated to taking on the toughest problems facing youth today.

- *Chaplaincy/Young Life Programs* offer Christ's message of hope, healing and wholeness to children who are recovering from the trauma of abuse and neglect.
- *Educational Support Services* provides ancillary support services to *Lighthouse Academy* and *Hope Academy of West Michigan.*
- *Employment Training Program* offers job skill training to residential youth and students at *Lighthouse Academy* and *Hope Academy of West Michigan*, preparing them for future employment.
- *Prevention Services* are designed to reduce teenagers' vulnerability to pregnancies, sexually transmitted diseases, substance use, violence, human trafficking and other high-risk behaviors.
- *Wellness and Camping Services* help address the emotional, mental and physical well being of residential clients through therapeutic and diverse experiences that create a sense of wholeness.
- Through the *Community Awareness and Education* component of Wedgwood's *Manasseh Project*, people in our community are empowered to end modern-day slavery.

Leadership and Volunteers

Wedgwood Christian Services employs approximately 400 staff and is led by a 16-member board. Wedgwood's Foundation is governed by a 10-member board.

Over 300 volunteers serve Wedgwood annually: in residential homes, volunteers and mentors assist in activities and share special gifts such as hairstyling, art projects and music; chaplain assistants lead Bible studies, and others volunteers assist with painting, woodworking and grounds work.

The caring women of Wedgwood's Guild shower kids with love on special occasions and honor graduates with cakes and parties. Guild members raise money for Wedgwood's *Chaplaincy Services*, making a crucial difference in providing spiritual support throughout the agency.

Vision

Wedgwood is committed to provide compassionate, Christian, professional and financially sustainable services for high-risk children and their families. For over 50 years the organization has diversified and adapted by responding to community needs. Wedgwood's "whole person" approach to treatment, encompassing emotional, physical, social, intellectual and spiritual needs, offers grace and healing to countless hurting young people.

Amy*
Residential Home for Girls

When Amy was twelve years old, her social worker told her she had burned every possible bridge. As a young girl she ran away from home and struggled with depression and drug use. She lacked stability, going from one shelter to another. In the 1980s Amy was referred to the former Wedgwood girls' home at 1245 Lake Drive in Grand Rapids. "A friend of mine who had been to Wedgwood forewarned me that this place was different," says Amy. "She said it was full of Jesus freaks and that residents did devotions and went to church, which was all very foreign to me."

"For most people, faith formation and spiritual development happen at home," says Emily VandenHeuvel, Chaplain Supervisor for Residential Services, "but many of these kids have been in and out of foster homes, and some have been abused by parents. Their perspective of spiritual concepts may be skewed because of what they've heard in the media."

Emily, along with Wedgwood's Spiritual Care Specialists and chaplains, offer hope and healing to hurting kids through Bible studies, devotions and one-on-one spiritual counseling in a loving, safe setting. Two worship services and Sunday School classes are offered each week at the Nagel Chapel in the center of Wedgwood's campus. In the same building, the Nagel Family Kids' Club is an inviting hub featuring comfy chairs, arcade games, Legos and art supplies. Clients can check out books, music CDs and DVDs from the library. At the Doug and Lois Nagel Gathering Grounds, clients can purchase snacks and drinks and enjoy the stereo and Wii system. Young Life holds events each Thursday in the chapel; clients also have the opportunity to attend off-campus camps and retreats.

Through Young Life and Wedgwood's Chaplaincy program, residents intentionally help others by serving meals at Dégagé Ministries, preparing Sack Suppers at Kids' Food Basket and creating cards and artwork for shut-ins. Spiritual care is voluntary, but over 75% of residents participate in prayer and spiritual activities. These programs are 100% funded by donor contributions. "Our kids are often at Wedgwood for a long time, which allows us to build relationships with them," says Emily. "We're open and nonjudgmental about where they are spiritually.

Since many clients are emotionally or developmentally impaired, it can be challenging to communicate the concepts of sin, forgiveness and grace. Chaplaincy staff have the delicate job of explaining that God created each person for a reason and that each one has a unique purpose.

"Many kids question why God would allow bad things to happen," says Emily. "They may have prayed time and time again for safety and a loving family, and they don't feel that God is listening. We teach them how to lament and grieve and that God grieves with them. It's painful, and it doesn't make sense, but God promises it won't be that way forever. The moments clients realize how valuable they are to God are incredibly exciting."

When Amy arrived at Wedgwood, she felt a sense of safety in the environment that she had not experienced elsewhere. "Even so," she says, "I continued to misbehave; one day I intentionally started a fire."

After she was sent back to Detroit, Amy's social worker informed her that no program would accept someone so troublesome. "During my time at Wedgwood," Amy says, "the counselors were compassionate, even when I was cruel. They told me I had so many gifts and that God had a plan for me. I thought about that a lot after I left, and I read the verses I'd marked in the Bible they gave me."

Amy began to believe that God had a purpose for her future and that she had a responsibility to do her part to fulfill it. She wrote letters to Wedgwood staff, apologizing for her behavior and asking for another chance. "I was fortunate," she says. "They took me back, and instead of preaching Christianity, they lived it. I felt even more secure because I could tell they genuinely cared. If they made mistakes they admitted it; I had never experienced such authenticity before."

Amy threw herself into the program, worked through issues successfully and had a family of her own. She went on to instill her deep faith into her five children. "Seeds are planted at Wedgwood," she says. "Devotions and church attendance were new to me, and I thought it was all about obeying rules and being disciplined. But at some point I began to forgive myself and see myself through God's eyes. Those words took root and grabbed hold of my heart years later."

After she left Wedgwood Amy earned her GED; she had always dreamed of becoming a doctor, but college seemed a lofty goal. When her youngest child was in kindergarten, she decided it was never too late. "Medical school was hard work, but I enjoyed every stage," she says. "Despite the long hours and intense work environment, I love being a doctor, and I feel I can make a difference when patients are going through traumatic experiences. I'm grateful I can show the same love to others that was shown to me all those years ago at Wedgwood."

*not her real name

Anthony
Parramore/VanderArk Homes

The Parramore Home has served as a secure residential facility on Wedgwood's campus since 1975. In 2011 Wedgwood responded to community needs by developing a program for some of Michigan's most vulnerable children. Parramore was designated to provide a safe, therapeutic home for those with a range of developmental disabilities. Seventeen-year-old Anthony was one of Parramore's first clients. Linda and her husband Gary fostered Anthony, who has autism, as a newborn and later adopted him. As a teen he became combative and aggressive and was not able to attend school. "Anthony had a hard time expressing emotions," says Linda. "He could show happiness, but every other emotion came out as anger." Anthony was begging for help, and after he was assessed at network180 he was placed at the Parramore Home.

"Making that decision was hard," continues Linda. "I cried for three weeks. But our lives had become so chaotic, and because we had existed day to day for so long, we didn't realize how dysfunctional our home life had become due to Anthony's behavior issues. It helped that Wedgwood staff was in constant communication with us; they were up front and honest, and we quickly realized that Anthony was where he needed to be."

"When a child on the autism spectrum has aggression issues," says Pat Pruiksma, Wedgwood Case Manager, "it can be difficult when there are siblings in the home. Removing the child from the home is a tough decision, but in the long run we can help the child because we've learned techniques that work. For example, sometimes parents may pacify a child with food when they become aggressive, but this only reinforces the behavior and teaches the child that aggression is an acceptable way to communicate their wants and needs. We teach the family when it's appropriate to strategically ignore certain behaviors and show them effective intervention methods."

Today both the Parramore and VanderArk homes offer individualized professional treatment for children and adolescents ages 7-18 with autism and other developmental disabilities. The program emphasizes the whole child including physical, emotional and spiritual well being. Staff includes a behavior analyst, speech and occupational therapists, and educational and medical personnel. "We work with organizations such as D.A Blodgett-St. Johns, network180 and Spectrum Community Services," says Pat. "When their service coordinators determine that residential care is the best option for the family, that's where we come in. Sometimes, when a family cannot meet the needs of a child, the court system refers them to us."

Wedgwood staff, referral agencies and parents determine when a child is ready to reunify with family. Some children stay only a few weeks, while others stay for over a year. Older clients may transfer to adult foster care facilities. "We want parents to know there is hope," says Pat. "Children with autism may have a different way of operating, but the kids we work with are loving and affectionate. Our goal is to support families and bring them together, and it's so rewarding to see growth in each child."

Many children in the homes are nonverbal. "A primary goal is to teach clients how to communicate their wants and needs," says Educational Specialist Genny Hinton, "either with picture systems, sign language or iPads. We've found that the ability to communicate reduces aggression."

Residents attend Lincoln Developmental Center and various public school Cognitively Impaired (CI) programs. Others attend Lighthouse Academy on Wedgwood's campus. "One of our jobs," says Genny, "is to bridge any gaps that may exist. It's important for teachers to know techniques we're utilizing to help the children progress, and we reinforce skills taught at schools." Additional areas of instruction include self-care skills, healthy leisure activities, safety skills and meal preparation. Children learn how to interact respectfully with others and build relationships.

During Anthony's nine months at Parramore, Linda, Gary and Anthony met with staff regularly to learn how to facilitate productive communication. Clear expectations were agreed upon for home visits, and consequences for misbehavior were outlined. Through behavior management training, Anthony learned to handle frustrations and take responsibility for his actions instead of blaming others. He is more aware of others' viewpoints and is quick to apologize for inappropriate behavior.

In August 2014 Anthony achieved a lifelong dream of riding in a hot air balloon.

Today Anthony, 20, looks forward to a driver's license, employment and his own apartment. "When Anthony was at Parramore," says Linda, "we realized that our family deserves to be calm and safe; Anthony knew his behavior needed to change before he could return home. He now has a future that will allow him freedoms the rest of us take for granted. I believe that Anthony was headed for a life of confinement, either in the penal system or in a restricted group home. I tell people that Wedgwood is a place that works miracles. Parramore saved Anthony's life."

Sarah*
Wedgwood's Manasseh Project

Wedgwood's Manasseh Project began shortly after professional staff at Wedgwood Christian Services helplessly watched as a child they knew and had cared for was trafficked and exploited in Grand Rapids. Despite efforts to find her and offer aid, they were unable and ill equipped to address her needs. Unwilling to stand still and watch this happen again, they researched the issue of sex trafficking and developed relationships with anti-trafficking organizations and law enforcement agencies in West Michigan. Wedgwood's Manasseh Project began in October 2012.

At Wedgwood's Manasseh Project Trauma Recovery Center, young women ages 12–17 are served with compassion and respect in a safe and therapeutic home environment. As the first home of its kind in Michigan, the staff develops relationships and provides enriching life experiences for these girls who have been robbed of their childhoods.

Personalized treatment is built on four pillars: therapy (individualized, group and activity-based), education, independent living skills and employment training. Clients' education is tailored to meet special needs through Lighthouse Academy. A beauty salon and sewing room provide opportunities to build community and self-esteem. Combined with Chaplaincy Services, holistic treatment is provided for the young women as they work toward healing.

Sex trafficking is defined as an act of recruiting or transporting a person through coercion for the purpose of sexually exploiting them into forced prostitution. The primary factor of vulnerability for sex trafficking of minors is the child's age; 13 years old is the average age of entry into prostitution. Children are especially susceptible due to the deception and manipulation of traffickers who recruit at schools, malls and parks. At least 100,000 American children are being exploited through pornography or prostitution every year. Research shows that one in three runaway kids will be approached by a trafficker within 48 hours. Especially at risk are kids in poor communities, where traffickers offer clothing, jewelry and cash in an effort to lure victims.

When Sarah was in middle school she lost interest in activities and became disconnected from friends. "In high school she became even more withdrawn," says Linda*, Sarah's mother. "Her outlet was the computer."

One evening, when Linda and Sarah attended a movie, Sarah left to use the rest room and did not return.

"I found out later that Sarah had arranged to meet someone she'd met on the Internet," says Linda. "I thought I'd never see her again. By the grace of God, she was found two weeks later."

After five months in a county facility, Sarah was still angry and bitter, adamant that she would not return home. "I knew things were not where they needed to be," says Linda, "so I pushed for more services. Wedgwood's Manasseh Project was just what Sarah needed."

Through intensive family therapy offered at Wedgwood's Manasseh Project Trauma Recovery Center, Sarah and her mother were able to develop mutual understanding and trust. They learned healthy ways to deal with anger, came to acknowledge the many ways they had hurt one another and worked toward forgiveness. A relationship that had seemed irrevocably broken began to heal. Through Lighthouse Academy, Sarah was able to graduate high school. She engaged in volunteer work with children and built a strong work ethic in Wedgwood's Employment Training Program. Sarah returned home to Linda, and is now working and enrolled in college.

"Sarah talks to me now, and I trust her," says Linda. "Counseling helped me see that I needed to change as a mom. I learned that I had to let go of my expectations and accept Sarah for who she was instead of trying to control her. I give a ton of credit to the therapists; they live out the philosophy of the program. Sarah believes she was created for the purpose of helping people, and I have no doubt she will achieve that goal."

Victims of sexual exploitation struggle to trust, love, make life decisions and succeed in a community. Sometimes the growth seen by staff is interpersonal, as with Sarah and Linda. In other cases young women learn to forgive themselves or see past experiences through a different, more accurate lens. Clients work through multiple traumas and experiences that seem too heavy to bear. Survivors not only heal in a safe environment, but also become advocates for others who have been victimized.

Through its Community Awareness and Education component, Wedgwood's Manasseh Project addresses the growing trend of sex trafficking in West Michigan by raising awareness and funding. While residential services are funded though public sources, Community Awareness and Education is funded 100% by donor contributions. Programming is established through collaborations with churches, local social groups, organizations, institutions of higher learning and businesses. By both offering healing to victims and educating families and the community, Wedgwood's Manasseh Project empowers the people of West Michigan to end modern-day slavery.

*not her real name

Lauren*
Intensive Outpatient Substance Abuse Program

Lauren began using alcohol when she 13 years old. "Life went completely downhill," she says. "I had no feelings and was numb to everything. I could only think about the next time I could get a fix." Soon Lauren was drinking every day. At 17 her alcohol use had led to several school suspensions, and she entered a residential rehabilitation center. From there, she came to Wedgwood's Intensive Outpatient Substance Abuse Program (IOP).

When she arrived, Lauren had been sober for 30 days, but she was still very fragile. Anthony Muller, Wedgwood Director of Clinical and Business Development and IOP therapist, describes the first time he saw Lauren. "Her emotions were all over the place," he says. "She had a lot of anger, but anger is a secondary emotion, which means there's something else (such as pain) that's fueling it. At first Lauren didn't even realize the extent of the abuse she'd experienced in the past."

Wedgwood's IOP serves adolescents ages 12-17. While substance abuse treatment had been a component of Wedgwood's residential program for decades, a need emerged for outpatient treatment for adolescents who lived at home. In 2000 the 17th District Court of Kent County received a grant and asked Wedgwood to provide substance abuse treatment to adolescents referred by the Court. Additional funding was received from network180, and private insurance agencies partnered as well. The IOP experienced rapid growth and was named Innovative Program of the Year in 2002 by the Michigan Federation for Children and Families.

At its inception, IOP clients were primarily referred by the court system, but Wedgwood's current client base is diverse. Some referrals are made by schools; when students are caught with substances, suspension periods may be cut in half if the student enters a treatment program. Doctors and psychiatric hospitals also make referrals.

Many IOP clients have a co-occurring condition such as depression or bipolar disorder. According to Muller, the face of adolescent addiction has changed dramatically in the last 18 years. "When I started at Wedgwood in 1996," he says, "the primary substances were alcohol and marijuana, and occasionally you'd get some kids who took pills. Since then there's been a huge push in ADHD diagnoses, and some kids use the medication to get high. There's also been an increase in pain medication prescriptions, and these are easy for kids to find.

"Another factor is innovation of substances," Muller continues. "At any given moment, someone is tweaking a substance in a lab. But the biggest influence has been medical marijuana because it changed kids' perception of harm. Many kids now think using marijuana and other substances is not such a big deal. Once the dam is opened you can't change perception."

Part of the reason for Wedgwood's IOP's success is the staff, many of whom have specialized in adolescent substance abuse for over 10 years. In addition, the IOP is uniquely designed for adolescents. In the first component of the program, adolescents come to group therapy three hours a day, three days a week. When sufficient progress is made, clients are engaged in substance abuse outreach therapy, typically with their families in their homes. The next step is individual outpatient counseling, followed by prevention services. This progression allows for an effective continuum of care.

"It comes down to being relevant," says Muller. "When kids work through activities during group time, not only does it build cohesion and energy, but kids see causes and effects for themselves. Motivational interviewing is also a big part of it."

In motivational interviewing, the adolescent sets life goals. The counselor gently helps the client self-reflect to discover that substance abuse is counter-intuitive to reaching those goals. "When kids discover the problem themselves," explains Muller, "they have ownership. If we tell them what they have to do, it puts up a barrier."

To offer another opportunity for Lauren to self-reflect, Muller gave her writing assignments. Now that she was sober, Lauren was able to think things through. She began to understand that her anger was rooted in the abuse she had experienced as a child. During outpatient counseling Lauren was willing to do the hard work of piecing together her painful memories. She realized that, haunted by these memories, drinking had been a way to avoid thinking and feeling. She opened up to her father, and together they successfully brought charges against Lauren's abuser.

"When I went through Wedgwood's program," says Lauren, "everyone was extremely accepting, and I had never experienced that before. The only emotion I expressed when I was using was anger, but today I can experience sadness without going to extreme lengths to block it out." Since leaving the IOP, Lauren has earned her high school diploma, and today she is a healthy young woman with a safe peer group.

Through Wedgwood's IOP over a hundred adolescents across Kent, Montcalm, Ottawa and Muskegon counties are guided on a path toward healing and recovery each year. "The reality is that adolescent substance abuse is not going away," says Muller. "It is also a reality that our passion and commitment to this population grows every year."

*not her real name

Diego and Kevin
Students, Hope Academy of West Michigan

When longtime therapist and educator Heidi Cate learned that over 200 students were expelled from Kent County schools each year she was deeply concerned. "Expelled students, by state law, cannot return to public schools for 180 days," Heidi says. "Within that time period, many students either drop out or become incarcerated." Heidi was moved to fill this critical gap by founding Lighthouse Academy in 2005. Today Lighthouse Academy, chartered by Ferris State University, offers renewed hope to about 400 young men and women each day across its five West Michigan sites.

"We focus on academic success," says Heidi, "but we also address whatever barriers stand in the way. Many students and their families have a deep-seated feeling of hopelessness because of stressors and traumas in their lives." Wedgwood staff realized there was a need to intervene deliberately to make sure students were "netted," or caught, before they came to Lighthouse. With this in mind, Hope Academy of West Michigan, a preschool-12th grade charter school, was opened in 2011 to serve students in the Garfield Park/Burton Heights neighborhoods of Grand Rapids.

Heidi, now the Superintendent of Lighthouse Academy and Hope Academy of West Michigan, explains what distinguishes these schools from others. "A foundational part of our programs," she says, "is that we invest in the whole child. Along with our primary core curriculum, a secondary curriculum incorporates life skills and social skills."

"A significant reason for our success," says Hope Academy of West Michigan's Principal Phillip Haack, "is that we hired the most effective teachers we could find. Small class sizes help us meet individual needs. At no point do we give up on a student; we look for ways to meet needs and pull in every possible resource." Students benefit from Wedgwood's wraparound services in which all members of the treatment community work toward a multidisciplinary plan to address academic, emotional, spiritual, mental and social well being. To take this a step further, the school's focus extends beyond the student to encompass the family's needs. Many families have multiple siblings at the school, which allows staff to create a community atmosphere and offer Wedgwood services to family members.

Diego transferred to Hope Academy of West Michigan in the middle of his kindergarten year. At his previous school he had spent his days in the resource room due to learning disabilities and a language impairment. Diego's transition was rough; his days were marked by frequent emotional outbursts and misbehavior. Within a week, the school's staff held a meeting with Diego's parents, who were supportive of testing and intervention.

Armed with a plan, Diego's classroom teacher, with help from the school's social worker and special education director, looked beyond Diego's behavior to understand possible triggers. They empowered him to identify

and work through frustrations, and he learned effective strategies for forming friendships. A speech pathologist helped him communicate his feelings, continuing comprehensive individual therapy throughout the summer. This team approach resulted in significant academic, social and emotional gains. Because he was now focused and engaged, Diego's first grade teacher, Alyssa Dean, discovered his exceptional math skills. Diego grew in confidence and self-awareness and persevered to meet reading goals. "It's amazing how much Diego has achieved," says Alyssa, "especially considering the hurdles he had to overcome to get there."

Kindergarten teacher Jill Jensen recalls another student's rocky beginning. "Kevin cried all day, every day," she says. "Then he started to act out violently. Since his English and Spanish language skills were not strong, he couldn't verbalize his feelings." The staff discovered that Kevin's mom

had been deported to Mexico. Jill was able to provide the daily structure and consistency that Kevin needed, and the entire staff rallied with their support. Kevin's classmates modeled their teacher's behavior by nurturing him and showing empathy. Kevin's mother returned, and by the end of the school year Kevin had developed into a natural leader.

"Kevin was like a different boy in first grade," says Alyssa. "He gave lots of hugs and fit in well with his peer group. Now, when he walks through the doors, he feels safe."

Committed parents show gratitude in many ways and are an integral part of the school's volunteer base. After working long hours at his job, Diego's father can often be found mopping the cafeteria. Kevin's mother recently offered a testimonial at a public meeting, describing what the school had done for her family. Hope Academy of West Michigan benefits from collaborative efforts with neighboring St. Francis Xavier Catholic Church, where many school families attend. Both institutions emphasize acceptance of all community members, persistence in times of conflict and mutual trust.

All partners converge and celebrate together at the spring graduation ceremony, where students speak of what it has meant to them to be a part of this vibrant community. At Hope Academy of West Michigan, barriers and generational cycles are broken, and families are empowered to envision their futures in a different way.

Home Repair Services

Resources for Home Owners

Mission: *Home Repair Services strengthens vulnerable Kent County homeowners because strong homeowners build strong communities.*

1100 S. Division Avenue
Grand Rapids, MI 49507
616.241.2601
homerepairservices.org

– Home Repair Services –

Roots

In the mid-1970s the Catholic Human Development Office began an emergency repair ministry in Grand Rapids to provide residents with functioning furnaces to warm their homes and sound roofs to keep them dry. Demand was high, so in 1979 Home Repair Services was spun off as a separate agency. A building that had been the site of Joppes Dairy at 1200 Jefferson Street became its first home.

At this time the City of Grand Rapids lent tools to homeowners, and in 1988 Home Repair Services was asked to take over this role. The *Tool Library* was born, allowing homeowners to borrow everything from lawn and garden implements to power tools. Through this venture, Home Repair Services staff encountered a new demographic of homeowners: people who were excited to tackle projects on their own. This realization was both eye opening and an exercise in humility, and it redefined the mission of Home Repair Services for years to come. Going forward, the organization would find ways to empower these resourceful homeowners to help themselves.

Plugging the Hole in the Bucket

Home Repair Services staff members believe that homeownership is a way to build value, dignity and pride, all essential components for neighborhood vitality. In vulnerable Grand Rapids neighborhoods, homeownership rates hover in the range of 30-50%, so those who are committed to owning and improving their own homes are the anchors that stabilize the neighborhood.

Dave Jacobs, Home Repair Services Executive Director since 1982, offers the analogy that raising the level of homeownership in central Grand Rapids is like trying to fill a leaky bucket. While some organizations provide pre-purchase support in order to add new homeowners to the bucket, Home Repair Services works exclusively to "plug the hole" with post-purchase homeownership services that help prevent the loss of more homeowners.

non profit
real estate developers

Home Repair
Services

A Focus on Vulnerable Homeowners

To meet low-income homeowners' material needs, Home Repair Services opened the *Builders' Abundance* store in 1992. Donated surplus materials–including recycled paint, lighting and plumbing fixtures, doors and windows–were sold to low-income homeowners at an affordable price.

In the same year Home Repair Services joined forces with the Home Builders Association of Greater Grand Rapids for *Community Repair Day*. In reality, this collaboration that continues to grow spans several months instead of one day. Construction crews volunteer their time and lumberyards donate materials for home access ramps.

Fix-It School classes were added in 1996, enabling homeowners to take on tough jobs such as drywall and plaster repair, tile and cabinet installation and electrical and plumbing systems. By decade's end the *Builders' Abundance* store was splitting at the seams; Home Repair Services needed a larger facility, and the Grand Rapids community rallied 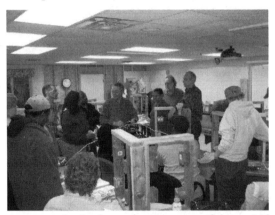 with support. Enough money was raised through a successful capital campaign in 1999 to purchase and renovate the former Mulvihill Oldsmobile dealership at 1100 S. Division Avenue. Partly as a response to the Grand Rapids community's generosity for their beautiful new facility, Home Repair Services continued to look for additional ways to serve vulnerable urban homeowners.

Because many children in low-income Grand Rapids homes were identified with elevated blood lead levels in 2000, Home Repair Services joined the national *CLEARCorp* collaborative to help educate the community about the issue. By 2006 the Grand Rapids community realized that lead poisoning in homes built before 1978 was still a pervasive concern, and the Healthy Homes Coalition (HHC) was born as a new agency.

Today Home Repair Services and HHC work in tandem to improve children's health by combatting hazardous conditions in the home. Asthma triggers identified by HHC such as mold, moisture and dust can be improved with proper ventilation, and Home Repair Services' *Air Sealing Program* provides improved ventilation as well as energy efficiency. Both organizations stress lead-safe work practices during remodeling projects.

Homeownership in the central city had decreased drastically due to urban sprawl in the '80s and '90s, but a different threat was ushered in with the new millennium in the form of a foreclosure crisis. Already in 2001, over 700 homes in Kent County were lost to foreclosure, and by 2008 that number had grown to 3,500. No other organization in the city was providing counseling services to stave off foreclosures, and since this was consistent with Home Repair Services' redefined mission, the *Foreclosure Intervention* program became Home Repair Services' next logical progression.

Within a few years a full-blown recession ensued and the foreclosure epidemic peaked, spreading from the city to the suburbs. The *Tool Library* and *Builders' Abundance* did not survive the recession, but Home Repair Services found a new and more cost–effective way to support do-it-yourselfers, and the *Remodeling Together* program was born.

Programs and Services

Since 1995 Home Repair Services has chosen one of its clients to receive the *Resourceful Homeowner Award*. At the annual celebration held in February, four finalists' stories are shared. Each homeowner has a unique story, but they all have many things in common: they are industrious, creative and determined. An award recipient is announced and cash prizes are distributed. All homeowners present are acknowledged for doing more than making a warm, safe place for family; they are commended for contributing enormously to the value of the neighborhood and to community stability.

More than 26,000 Grand Rapids area homeowners have received assistance from Home Repair Services over the years. While many Home Repair Services efforts could be classified as "community development," an even greater focus is on social services. Home Repair Services has always been more interested in the person than the house.

Home Repair Services facilitates in the building of about 50 wheelchair ramps each year for people with mobility constraints and disabilities.

Repair Program: Professional service technicians on the *Repair Team* handle urgent and critical problems for qualifying lower-income homeowners. Residents with mobility impairments can apply to the *Home Access Ramps* program for assistance with wheelchair ramps or bathroom modifications. When a client's mobility is challenged, physical therapists from Disability Advocates go into the home to determine which modifications are most beneficial to the family.

Home energy auditors from the *Air Sealing Program* help lower-income homeowners find and seal air leaks, which result in better ventilation, lower gas bills and improved health. Since most older homes have little or no insulation, the program also insulates attics and sidewalls; for a relatively low cost, homeowners realize remarkable energy savings.

Self-Help Program: The *Remodeling Together* program uses an application and selection process to pair lower-income homeowners with experienced coaches to tackle kitchen and bathroom projects. Coaches spend up to 30 hours of one-on-one time with homeowners, offering guidance in project design, budgeting, material selection and installation. Qualifying homeowners who are interested in tackling a kitchen or bathroom themselves can purchase affordable cabinets.

Fix-It School classes are available to all, regardless of income level. Since clients are not always able to attend classes to learn remodeling skills, Home Repair Services provides a catalog of nearly 200 do-it-yourself videos, accessible on the website. The videos feature some of the do-it-yourself industry's most respected and well-known experts.

Financial Counseling Program: Counseling is available to avert foreclosures, improve credit ratings and review refinancing transactions. United Way, recognizing that housing is a basic human need, provides funding to Home Repair Services' *Foreclosure Intervention* program.

Money Matters classes offer solutions to common challenges and establish a firm financial foundation. Classes are offered in English and Spanish; they are free and open to everyone, regardless of income. Topics include credit repair, foreclosure prevention and insurance.

Funding

President Gerald Ford enacted the Federal Community Development Block Grant in 1974 to help extinguish poverty and urban blight. When Home Repair Services was begun in 1979, the City of Grand Rapids immediately began a tradition of sharing some of its block grant allocation, and the City of Wyoming and Kent County followed suit. This program has steadily been reduced; in 2011-2012 Home Repair Services lost $250,000 of this funding.

Kent County taxpayers approved the Kent County Senior Millage in 1999, which recognized the importance of critical repairs and wheelchair ramps. Despite declining property tax values, it continues to provide more than $300,000 annually toward these repairs.

Home Repair Services has many faithful friends who, for many years, have collectively contributed about $500,000 a year. Volunteers and donors of goods and services contribute in important ways. Most of Home Repair Services' projects are offered as affordable financial transactions; homeowners typically contribute about 10% to the annual budget.

Leadership and Volunteers

Home Repair Services employs 22 staff members, organized into several departments. Financial counselors are well trained and certified at the federal and state levels. Tradespeople from various sectors of the building industry lend their expertise in repairing homes and coaching do-it-yourselfers. AmeriCorps provides funding to maintain a *Foreclosure*  *Intervention* intake specialist. All services are offered in English and Spanish. Twelve individuals serve on the Home Repair Services Board.

More than 300 people volunteer each year at Home Repair Services. *Fix-it School* instructors share structural knowledge and project experience; talented retirees work alongside staff, and the Home Builders Association of Greater Grand Rapids donates about $40,000 of labor and materials toward wheelchair construction every year.

Vision

The Home Repair Services staff like to remind themselves that if they do the mission well day in, day out, year after year, Kent County will experience "confident homeowners enjoying vibrant communities." That's the vision that propels their work.

Jason Paulateer
Homeowner, Past Board Member

As an employee of NBD Bank in 1997, Jason Paulateer noticed a posting in the branch lobby. Home Repair Services, just down the street, was offering classes to anyone who wanted to learn the basics of home remodeling. Newlyweds Jason and Chapri signed up for a variety of classes.

Armed with their new knowledge, the couple's first project was to rip everything out of their bathroom except for the tub. They then installed a new vanity and sink, revamped the plumbing and electrical fixtures, added a dropped ceiling, re-glazed the tub and installed a new subfloor and ceramic tile. The Paulateers were proud of the results and looked around for another project to tackle.

Chapri ran a daycare center from their home. With their newfound skills, they built a retaining wall on the slope of the backyard and built a fence around the perimeter so the children could have a safe place to play.

Over the years, because of what they learned at Home Repair Services, Jason and Chapri completely transformed their home. They learned firsthand about pride of ownership and achieved a tremendous sense of accomplishment. They referred many people to Home Repair Services and remained connected by making donations and attending the organization's functions.

Still in his 20s, Jason found a way to give back by serving on the board. "I learned about board governance and how to run meetings," says Jason, "but more than anything, I learned that there are many good people out there. Home Repair Services has always been very intentional about diversity, not only in regard to the people they serve, but also in regard to the people who serve on the board."

During his tenure, Jason served with a builder, a developer, a bank executive and a nun. "I was by far the youngest board member," he recalls, "and I was a sponge. The things I learned at that table are foundational to the person I am today. I learned what it takes to make wise decisions. At times there were people who tried to make Home Repair Services something it's not, but Home Repair Services has always been deliberate about "staying in their lane." Their mission is to help low-income families keep their homes, and they are very clear about that goal."

Even after his tenure on the board expired in 2005, Jason continued to attend the annual Resourceful Homeowner Celebrations and served one year on the selection committee. "One of the things that stood out every year," he says, "was that people who barely had two pennies to scrape together were so giving of themselves. Many of the stories at that time had to do with low-income families either fostering, adopting or somehow bringing additional kids into their families and homes, and then tapping into Home Repair Services as a way to maintain that life."

Five years ago Jason and Chapri adopted five children. "I have to believe that those early years at Home Repair Services played into our decisions somehow," he says.

Jason believes that, if it were not for Home Repair Services, Grand Rapids would have been hit much harder by the recent real estate crisis. "Because Home Repair Services focused on the post-purchase market segment," he explains, "the leadership team always kept an eye on foreclosure numbers across the country. When (Executive Director) Dave Jacobs noticed an uptick in Michigan foreclosures, the board made decisions that enabled the organization to get in front of the problem so people could keep their homes. They hired more counselors and helped all residents, regardless of income or circumstances."

What began as a leadership decision to concentrate on homeownership financial counseling morphed into an effective foreclosure prevention program at the peak of the crisis. Currently at Home Repair Services, foreclosure intervention counseling is provided to approximately 700 homeowners each year.

Photo Courtesy of The Detroit News

Jason and Chapri, along with their eight children, currently live in Troy, Michigan. Jason is Vice President and Market Manager at PNC Community Development Banking, which is also devoted to improving low-to-moderate income neighborhoods. "The lessons I learned at Home Repair Services are the fabric of my life," says Jason. "Even though some people in their respective stations may have more access to resources, deep down inside we are all the same. And I learned that people give when they are given to.

Gabrielle Luster
Remodeling Together

When Gabrielle Luster was a renter, she stopped at Home Repair Services one day out of curiosity. There she learned that they offered classes to teach homeowners do-it-yourself techniques, and she signed up for Money Matters. Gabrielle soon realized that by paying rent she was not building equity, and she became determined to buy her own home. A few years later she made that dream come true and became fully invested in everything Home Repair Services had to offer. Her first project was her kitchen. To start, Gabrielle attended Fix-It School classes and watched videos from the Tool Library. With the help of her uncle and her son, Troy, she tore out the old cabinets.

Then Gabrielle's uncle passed away in 2003. "I was angry about my uncle's death and I needed to focus on something," she says. Gabrielle tore into the project as a way of dealing with her grief. Using ceramic tile from Builders' Abundance and with guidance from a remodeling coach, she built a new kitchen countertop. When she could not find the right paint color in local stores, the HRS staff helped her mix colors to formulate the perfect shade. The cabinets that Gabrielle installed came from several batches of donations, expertly matched by Builders' Abundance staff. A doorway into the basement from the kitchen was closed off and a new doorway was built in the dining room.

HRS Education Coordinator Judy Jordan encouraged Gabrielle to take part in the initial pilot project for the Pride of Ownership (which later evolved into the Remodeling Together) program, funded by the Grand Rapids Foundation. She took some women-only classes, refitted the plumbing and installed recessed lighting. BJ Jordan, HRS Self-Help Program Manager, provided invaluable guidance as Gabrielle installed floor tiles, which she describes as "putting together a jigsaw puzzle."

For her successful kitchen remodeling project, Home Repair Services nominated Gabrielle for the Resourceful Homeowner Award in 2005, but another finalist came away with the top award. Undeterred and energized by learning new techniques and by recycling materials, her remodeling extended to other areas her home. She updated the electric system in her cozy family room and refinished the stairs.

Then Gabrielle lost her job in 2010. "I felt like a nothing as a mom because I couldn't provide for my son," she says. "But Judy and BJ provided gift cards so I could purchase Christmas gifts for Troy. They showed such kindness and knew that my dignity was important."

Gabrielle rechanneled her frustration and took it out on her kitchen wall. A pass-through to the dining room was created in its place, along with an inviting snack bar. Damaged plaster was removed, and new drywall was hung, taped, mudded and painted.

Old carpet was removed throughout the house, and because of the expense of renting a sander, Gabrielle sanded and refinished the floors by hand. After studying more videos, she and Troy framed in the basement walls, added insulation and hung new drywall. They installed new plumbing, changed electrical outlets and ventured into carpentry. Through the Air Sealing Program, many air leaks were found around door and window frames. Caulking these leaks and adding insulation made her home more energy efficient. Gabrielle's hard work paid off. She was again a finalist in 2011, and this time was named Resourceful Homeowner of the Year.

These accomplishments have helped Gabrielle to grow in many ways. "I used to be an introvert, but now I have the confidence to step out and be more vocal. I don't hesitate to refer neighbors and friends to Home Repair Services." She estimates that over 50% of the people in her neighborhood have had assistance from Home Repair Services, which has created a surge in home values, aesthetics and pride of ownership. "I learned that I am Superwoman," says Gabrielle. "I'm not afraid to ask questions and I'm not intimidated when faced with new challenges." She also learned the importance of focusing on the needs of others, giving back by teaching several Fix-It School classes at Home Repair Services and at her church. When Gabrielle's brother died in 2006, her family developed Moise's Minds, an organization that raises money to provide backpacks and school supplies for children. Through the support of several Home Repair Services staff members and the community, this organization has earned money to furnish hundreds of filled backpacks each year.

Today, entering Gabrielle's home is like opening a decorator's magazine. "I could never have remodeled my home without Home Repair Services," says Gabrielle. "Truthfully, I probably wouldn't have been able to keep my home if it weren't for the counseling I received when times were

tough. When people lose their jobs they become dejected, but Financial Counseling allows people to keep their homes. Home Repair Services is not just about providing supplies, it's about building community. It gives people hope, and it's a safe place because the staff shows respect to everyone who walks through the door."

Gabrielle's wish is for a broader awareness of how Home Repair Services benefits the Grand Rapids community, and that more people will volunteer their skills. "If I won the lottery, I would give it all to Home Repair Services," she says. And she means it.

The VanRooyen Family
Home Access Ramp

"Our life has been a series of miracles," says Nancy VanRooyen. She counts among them the wheelchair ramp that was built for her family by Home Repair Services in August 2013.

Nancy and her husband, Paul, have three children: Katie (7), Josh (5) and Eric (3). Soon after Paul and Nancy brought Josh home from the hospital he began to have seizures. Tests revealed that he had elevated glycine levels, and he was diagnosed with nonketotic hyperglycinemia, or NKH, a rare genetic disorder caused by the shortage of an enzyme, which causes a buildup of glycine. This impacts brain function, and as a result Josh's mobility is restricted; he rolls and scoots but does not walk unassisted, so he uses a wheelchair. His cognitive functioning is comparable to that of a 10-month-old. Josh's vision is impaired, and he must be tube-fed.

When Nancy was pregnant with Eric, prenatal tests revealed that he, too, had NKH. Because of early detection and intervention he has made considerable progress. Although Eric could walk with the aid of leg braces, now Paul and Nancy had two children who could benefit from a ramp to ease their mobility.

While Josh's attendance at Lincoln Developmental Center provides a much-needed break in routine, lifting the wheelchair up and down the steps by the front door and transporting him back and forth was becoming more of a challenge for Nancy, who has scoliosis. "Lifting the wheelchair one step at a time is tough on your back, and it will get more challenging as Josh grows," says Paul. "There's always the danger of slipping, especially when there's rain or snow."

Paul and Nancy looked into building a ramp and found the cost to be exorbitant. Then Paul's mom suggested they contact Home Repair Services, and Nancy made the phone call.

"I thought that Home Repair Services only built ramps for senior citizens," she says. "But we filled out some paperwork and soon we learned that we qualified for the ramp. The staff were extremely gracious and accommodating Before we knew it, a crew came out to take measurements and draw up a plan. Their goal was to finish the ramp before the new school year."

The VanRooyens' ramp was built as part of Community Repair Day, a collaborative effort that has existed for over two decades between Home Repair Services and the Home Builders Association of Greater Grand Rapids (HBAGGR). Employees from local construction companies volunteer time and area lumber yards donate materials. For many years, Community Repair Day was observed on the second Saturday in September, but some builders had a conflict with the date. Now projects are spread out over the summer and fall, allowing builders and volunteers to choose the date that works best for them. Before the work begins, Disability Advocates of Kent County visit the home site to ensure the ramp meets specifications.

When the crew from Roersma and Wurn Builders began work at the VanRooyen home, a woman from the neighborhood stopped by to share how Home Repair Services had offered assistance years ago to her mother in their home just a few houses down the street. Many others have since shared stories about Home Repair Services with Paul and Nancy.

The work didn't stop when the ramp was completed. The people at Home Repair Services know that pride of ownership encompasses an entire home, inside and out, so they arranged for landscape improvements. A group of volunteers from U.S. Signal, a local communications company, came to the VanRooyen home on a cold and rainy day to clean up the yard and perform landscaping. Further modifications were made inside the home to make it easier to transport Josh.

"The ramp saved my back," says Nancy. "Now it's relatively easy to get the kids in and out the door. Going for a walk or visiting the park is no longer a major undertaking, and we have more freedom."

"We can't do this alone," adds Paul. "Sometimes it's the little things that make a big difference. Everyone from Home Repair Services was so respectful. Volunteers saw the needs and offered their time and energy with no strings attached. Making that one phone call changed our lives."

Steve Sielaff
Volunteer Remodeling Coach

Steve Sielaff has worked in the building and remodeling field his entire life. In the 1970s he had a crew of twenty men in Warren, Michigan, working for him. In the '80s he moved to Houston, Texas, and started over again, experiencing similar success. He moved to Denver, Colorado, in the '90s and again his business thrived.

When Steve returned to Michigan in 2000 to be closer to family, it was apparent that the state's economy had changed drastically in the two decades he had lived elsewhere. Businesses were suffering, population had decreased and jobs were hard to come by. Steve discovered firsthand the devastation of the building industry, yet he had always bounced back before and assumed things would improve.

After some tough years of sporadic projects and buying materials on credit, Steve's assets were depleted and he and his wife Karen lost their home. Steve had never imagined himself living in a single-wide trailer, but his new reality gave him a different perspective.

Having spent much of his career remodeling HUD properties for low-income families, Steve had seen how difficult it was for many to make ends meet. "My attitude was that these people were ungrateful and taking a handout," he admits. "Like many people, when you're doing well and you see people who are struggling, I used to think *at least they could get a job at McDonalds.* But when I had problems of my own, I could see exactly how people got where they were. For the first time in my life my heart went out to them."

In addition to financial burdens, Steve was also experiencing serious health issues. In the 1990s he suddenly lost strength in his arms and legs. For years the doctors could not determine the reason, but one theory was that he had been exposed to chemicals. Part of Steve's treatment was chemotherapy, which made him susceptible to broken bones. For a time he was wheelchair-bound, but even then he did not miss a day of work.

"Instead of thinking *woe is me* I figured God had a plan for me that I just hadn't figured out," says Steve. "He was pressing on me to do something, and I thought I could help people with the knowledge I had obtained over the years when work was plentiful. I asked the City of Grand Rapids where I could volunteer, and they suggested Home Repair Services." Karen, who has been with him every step of the way, encouraged him to give back.

For the first time Steve was remodeling to help people, not for monetary gain. It was also the first time he had to accept help from others, but serving others took his mind off his own circumstances. Steve has taught dozens of Fix-It School classes and served as a coach on many Remodeling Together projects. His first coaching client was a single mom who ran a daycare in her home, yet still managed to maintain her home beautifully.

"I'd get her started and let her go," he explains. "When I'd visit the next day she'd have the job done, and it was always done well. That's more than I can say for lots of the contractors I've dealt with. She changed my whole way of thinking. She had so many strikes against her, but she didn't let anything stand in her way. Whatever roadblock she encountered, she dealt with it and moved on. I was amazed by her determination and impressed by her work ethic.

"It dawned on me," Steve continues, "that if I felt that good helping someone else, why would I not want someone else to feel that way if they helped me? I never met anyone at Home Repair Services who treated me like I was handicapped. They show respect to everyone, they think the best of people and they don't judge. They live out their faith by the way they treat people. Sometimes when you help people for a while, you lose compassion. But the folks at Home Repair Services don't."

Steve also learned that success can be measured in many different ways. "Remodeling a kitchen may not be a big deal for some, but for people who are struggling, it may be at the top of their bucket list. These people were happy in their simple lifestyle and were satisfied and rewarded by this simple kitchen. I could have done the work for them, but then they wouldn't have any personal reward. I'd lay materials out and keep the homeowners on track. By pushing them beyond what they thought they were capable of, they felt a sense of accomplishment."

Volunteering has also opened doors for Steve. "I put an ad on craigslist to offer my guidance in remodeling jobs, and the response has been amazing. I don't charge much, and just like in my volunteer work at Home Repair Services, I mostly give direction; the homeowners get to take pride in their own work. It's reward enough for me to get the interaction and feedback.

"I am being totally honest when I say that I get more out of my volunteer work than what I give," Steve continues. "My faith has been strengthened through my work with Home Repair Services, and I've experienced gratitude like never before. I'm not at all living in luxury now, but this is where I'm supposed to be at this moment. And I'm thankful to have met such awesome people because of what I went through."

Christy Perez
Remodeling Together

For many years Christy Perez kept an envelope with clippings and photographs of home remodeling ideas. Labeled simply "My Dream House," the envelope was a source of inspiration and a ready resource when opportunities presented themselves. A photograph depicting gleaming hardwood floors inspired her to remove old carpet and stain the floors of her living room. Energized by what she had accomplished, Christy was ready to tackle her kitchen, the hub of her home.

Christy is grateful that she was at the right place at the right time in 2007 when she came to Home Repair Services. Self-Help Program Manager BJ Jordan asked her if she would like to participate in the newly formed Remodeling Together program. A coach would assist with layout design and get her started, but the rest would be up to her. Christy was ready with a picture of her dream kitchen and plenty of enthusiasm.

"My coach would spend two or three hours at my house each time, showing me how to drywall, tile the floor and install plumbing and lights. Then he'd leave and let me do it on my own."

Christy's budget did not allow for cabinets from a big name store, but Home Repair Services presented an affordable option—because of donated materials and volunteer labor, inexpensive cabinets were available for anyone who wanted to do their own stain and varnish work.

"I'm a hair stylist, not a carpenter," remarks Christy, "but I had to grab this opportunity. My three kids knew I was serious when I gutted my entire kitchen down to two-by-fours and wires, and they helped me put it all back together again." Her daughter helped stain and varnish the cabinets, a son in college painted the breakfast nook and a son serving in Afghanistan installed crown molding and door trim when he came home on leave.

Christy installed new drywall on the kitchen ceiling, a task made particularly difficult because of arthritis in her back. It was hot summer work, requiring overhead patching and sanding after a full day at her job. Undeterred, Christy completed the project herself. She installed a granite countertop, updated electrical outlets and added ceramic tile flooring. And she challenged her Home Repair Services remodeling coach, too. Feeling confident with her ceramic tile installation skills, she insisted on a diagonal pattern for her backsplash. New appliances made the kitchen picture-perfect; her kitchen looked almost exactly like the picture she

had clipped from the magazine years ago.

Tackling the remodeling of her kitchen allowed Christy to become self-sufficient. "I learned how strong I really am. I used to be very impatient, and this taught me to be more focused and determined for the big reward in the end," she says. Making these improvements enhanced Christy's pride of ownership, and it also greatly increased the resale value of her home. Research shows that improvements in kitchens and bathrooms are often the best investments homeowners can make.

Now Christy is confident enough to help neighbors with their repairs. And a hair stylist gets to spend lots of time with a captive audience. "Most of my clientele know my story. I have lots of opportunities to tell them about Home Repair Services when they need help or if they're looking for a place to volunteer."
Christy's clients tease her by saying that she became an overnight sensation when Home Repair Services sent direct mail postcards advertising the Remodeling Together program to a wide distribution area in Grand Rapids and the surrounding communities. The postcards featured a picture of Christy with hand on hip, beaming as she stood next to her gorgeous granite countertops.

"I believe that God puts people where they need to be," says Christy, "and he brought a lot of good people in my path. I formed bonds with the Home Repair Services staff and construction coaches, and they became my extended family. It opened my eyes to have a bigger understanding of other people. We don't really know what people are going through, but when they're doing what they love and helping others it makes them feel better."

The example set by Home Repair Services staff and volunteers motivated Christy to find ways to pay it forward. "If anyone mentions issues about their homes," she says, "my ears perk up and I ask what I can do to help because I was so touched by what was done for me. Of course I tell people about Home Repair Services every chance I get. If I hadn't bumped into BJ Jordan that day, I am convinced that I'd still be looking at magazines, and my kitchen would never have been transformed. Homeownership is the best thing since chocolate. And you're getting that from a woman!"

Kids' Food Basket

Mission: *Attacking childhood hunger to help young people learn and live well*

2055 Oak Industrial Drive, Suite C
Grand Rapids, MI 49505
616.235.4532
kidsfoodbasket.org

– Kids' Food Basket –

Roots

In 2000 MaryAnn Prisichenko, a building principal for the Grand Rapids Public Schools, discovered a little girl digging through the trash looking for food. MaryAnn began to search for an organization that could help ensure her students received adequate nutrition after school. When Mary K. Hoodhood, Manager of Volunteer Services at a local nonprofit, heard this she thought, "We need to feed these kids."

With a broad, deep base of contacts and support in Grand Rapids from her previous twenty years as a volunteer coordinator, along with the fact she couldn't sleep at night until she did something to solve this problem, Mary K. began a small program to feed children in the fall of 2001. From these roots came the idea of Kids' Food Basket, which was officially founded in 2002.

No one likes to think of children going hungry, and donations began to trickle in to the tune of $3,000 the first year. That small budget, plus a relationship nurtured with the West Michigan Food Bank, put a Sack Supper—a brown bag containing a meat-and-cheese sandwich, a piece of fruit, a granola bar and a juice box—into the hands of 125 children every weekday at three schools.

Founder Mary K. Hoodhood with Principal MaryAnn Prisichenko and Sibley Elementary students

A Decade of Growth

A second stage of growth for Kids' Food Basket began a few years later when the operation, which had been running out of a few church basements, moved into a 1,100 square foot facility. The number of volunteers increased, another staff person was hired, and more information was learned about hunger. Teachers credited Sack Suppers with improving the concentration levels of their students, trust was built with the kids, an advisory committee was formed and creativity was used to overcome obstacles. Still, funding only came from a small—yet growing—community of friends and volunteers. The word spread.

The "tipping point" for Kids' Food Basket was 2008, as the organization finally garnered the attention of the community and powers

that be. As awards were won and recognition for Kids' Food Basket grew, donations multiplied and funding was now granted from larger foundations and organizations that hadn't deemed the effort "sustainable" in the past. The result was that more schools on the waiting list could be served Sack Suppers; growth was 59% in 2009 and a whopping 62% in 2010.

Now in its fourth phase, the past few years have shown a strong and sustainable organization. As of Fall 2014, the budget was $3.9 million, the staff numbered 17, and more than 6,300 children at 33 sites in Grand Rapids and Muskegon were given a Sack Supper to take home at the end of each school day. In addition, a summer program serves hundreds of kids.

Sack Suppers

Each day, five days a week, some 200 volunteers pack and deliver Sack Suppers, which contain food from all five food groups. Snack packs are also included on Fridays to provide weekend nutrition. In the schools served, 90% or more of the student population qualify for free or reduced lunches. Even with this requirement, there is consistent demand for Kids' Food Basket's services, and there are a number of schools on the waiting list at any given time. *(Note: The number of children fed, schools served and volunteers engaged continually grows.)*

Sack Suppers are a victory in the attack on childhood hunger. When paired with breakfast and lunch at school, they meet daily recommended nutritional requirements for children. Such a simple program has such a powerful impact because it gives kids the stability to stay focused, get their homework done on a full stomach and stay on track academically. The role of Kids' Food Basket is critical because today 42,974 children living in Kent and Muskegon Counties are food insecure—a term defined as the lack of access at all times to enough food for an active, healthy life, with no need for recourse to emergency food sources or other extraordinary coping behaviors. Another way to look at it is: one in four Michigan kids suffers from hunger every day. By age 12, any physical damage sustained from malnourishment is irreversible. Kids' Food Basket provides children with an important tool—a nutritious meal—to ensure they become healthy, self-sufficient adults.

Funding

About 40% of the food provided in each Sack Supper is obtained from Feeding America West Michigan Food Bank, formerly Second Harvest Gleaners. Their food items cost 16 cents per pound. Another 40% of the food provided is donated by area grocery stores and food vendors. For example, all of the bread for Sack Supper sandwiches is donated by Bimbo Bakery. The other 20% is received through food drives and the generous support of the community.

Kids' Food Basket is funded entirely through charitable donations; no federal, state, county or city monies are received. Numerous businesses and community service clubs host fundraisers each year to support the mission.

A unique aspect of Kids' Food Basket is its *Kids Helping Kids* program whereby youngsters volunteer their time in some way for the effort to end hunger. One example is a recent flurry of events where students from Comstock Park Public Schools held a juice box drive at each school, sold tee shirts, held an orange-out basketball game and participated in "Go Orange for Hunger Day." Through their many efforts 1,715 pounds of juice and $1,825 were donated.

Staff

Kids' Food Basket has a small paid staff, including Executive Director Bridget Clark Whitney, who has been with the organization since its inception. "Bridget took my idea and turned it into a highly respected organization," says founder Mary K. Hoodhood. "She is an energetic, passionate individual who has grown into a skilled professional. Because Bridget has engaged the Grand Rapids community in such a positive way, we have been able to make a difference in the well being of our area children. Under Bridget's leadership, Kids' Food Basket has undergone significant growth, from serving 250 children in 2002 to 6,300 children each weekday in 2014. The annual budget has skyrocketed from $20,000 to $3.9 million."

In addition to staff, Kids' Food Basket is guided by a board of directors and 13 committees/task forces to meet strategic goals. For board members to be fully versed in Kids' Food Basket's daily operations and culture, he or she must have volunteered a minimum of six months before becoming a board member. The growth of Kids' Food Basket could not have happened without the energy, support and love of thousands of volunteers.

Youth Grants Committee volunteers

High Honors

Physical limitations have not hindered Mary K.'s determination to uplift her community. Though a 1980 car accident left her paralyzed, she was determined her disability was not going to define or deter her. Described by friends and colleagues as "bold, fearless, audacious, an instigator and one who never accepts 'no' for an answer," Mary K. recognizes strengths in others and brings out the best in them.

In addition to many local awards and recognition, Mary K. was presented the U. S. Presidential Citizen's Medal from President Barak Obama in August 2010 for her extraordinary efforts to nourish children. The award is the second highest honor a citizen can receive and recognizes individuals who have performed exemplary deeds or services for his or her country or fellow citizens. Also in 2010 Kids' Food Basket received the Governor's Service Award for *Best Volunteer Program* in the state of Michigan AND Bridget was a national fellow for *Next Generation Leaders* through Independent Sector.

Kids' Food Basket has received numerous awards, including the 2014 "Nonprofit of the Year" by the Grand Rapids Area Chamber of Commerce.

Vision

The fight to end childhood hunger becomes more significant during tough economic times. To fully serve Kids' Food Basket's mission of *ending* hunger, its current, three-year strategic initiatives are:

- Improve and grow the attack locally
- Build a movement beyond Kent County
- Empower youth as part of the attack
- Reflect community members of all backgrounds

Childhood hunger denies dignity, robs kids of physical and mental energy and undermines community stability. The *Nourish Challenge* campaign was launched in 2014 to raise additional funds to provide more fresh fruits and vegetables in Sack Suppers. It partners with local farmers and wholesalers to ensure every Sack Supper has the brain food kids need. Another recent initiative is to assist and model the Kids' Food Basket program to other communities around the country.

Since its inception, three themes have remained constant for Kids' Food Basket: there are lots of hungry kids in the community, thus an overwhelming need for its services; the organization is making an impact, making a difference; and there are continuing leadership lessons to be learned. The emphasis has shifted from social justice to love.

One of Executive Director Bridget Clark Whitney's credos is, "Don't overthink it, just figure it out," which has stood the organization in good stead while maintaining the delicate balance of grassroots work and explosive growth. But perhaps the key to the phenomenal success of Kids' Food Basket is this thought: "While poverty is complex, feeding a hungry child is not."

Cindi Welton
Board Member

Fifth Third Bank Vice President Cindi Welton first learned about Kids' Food Basket when she was invited to a "Lunch and Learn" at the B.O.B. in 2005 by her colleague Dan Oumedian. Dan's father Armen was an early contributor of seed funding for the program and Dan was helping spread the word. "I fell in love with the mission of Kids' Food Basket," says Cindi. "It matched my passion to feed hungry kids."

Cindi initially volunteered to become a "Crew Facilitator," meaning she supervised the sandwich making and packing of Sack Suppers every third Thursday of the month after work. Over 100 volunteers throughout the day make sandwiches and pack Sack Suppers to produce the daily 6,000 that are distributed to schools throughout the city.

"Over the years, I have reached out to my Fifth Third colleagues, encouraging them to participate, and now about 40% of my crew is made up of fellow bank employees," says Cindi. In addition to inspiring forty co-workers to volunteer, Cindi's uncle and aunt, Larry and Paula Strockis, are now crew facilitators and strong supporters of Kids' Food Basket, along with their grandkids.

About six months later, founder Mary K. Hoodhood asked Cindi if she was willing to join a committee. "I can't say 'no' to Mary K.," Cindi says, and she soon became part of the 12-person Fund Development Committee whose main goal is to keep the doors open with a steady stream of donations.

One outgrowth of the Fund Development Committee is the *Kids Helping Kids* program, whereby a staff person visits the schools to raise money and encourage food drives. "Last year a student at Union High School came up to one of our staff and said he had been a recipient of Sack Suppers," says Cindi. "He said if we hadn't been there for him with the meals, he didn't think he'd be where he is today—learning, playing sports, and on-track to graduate from high school. We get letters of thanks from students and teachers on a regular basis. It's very gratifying."

After six months on the committee, Mary K. again approached Cindi and asked her to consider becoming a member of the board. "I was honored to accept," says Cindi.

She is currently in her fifth year on the 12-person board, and is intellectually stimulated by the diverse backgrounds and collected wisdom of the members which include a former Grand Rapids Public Schools principal, a gastroenterologist, another banker, a project manager from Amway Corporation, a design artist from Herman Miller, a lawyer, a public relations person and a public policy and development specialist from Spectrum Health who used to work in Washington, D.C.

"All these people are passionate, wise and engaged, and we have rich discussions. We have the momentum to keep the Kids' Food Basket mission growing. It's also a tribute to Mary K., who is an inspiration to us all. We don't want to let her down," continues Cindi.

Cindi loves that the board is extremely engaged in the mission and the outcome of the mission. "We make the sandwiches, pack the Sack Suppers and deliver them. We attend events where the teachers come up to us and say, 'The kids aren't falling asleep in class anymore. Their test scores are improving.' It's so affirming for us." Board members also interact with staff members to empower them in their roles.

Currently, Cindi volunteers about 30 hours a month with her various commitments as Crew Facilitator, Fund Development Committee member, Expansion Committee member, Board Governance Committee Chair, and Executive Committee Board Vice President.

Kids' Food Basket has enhanced Cindi's life. She says, "It's fun, exciting and rewarding. The mission is simple: feed hungry kids. When you make a sandwich and pack the brown bag supper, you know that tomorrow a hungry child will eat that meal. Each will be fed and able to reach their greatest potential. Knowing that such immediate and profound impact is improving the lives of children in our community inspires me and each volunteer."

Nancy Hamstreet
School Social Worker

As a school social worker, Nancy Hamstreet often had students come to her office during the day, asking for snacks. "They told me they were hungry," says Nancy. "We provide breakfast and lunch for most, yet they were still hungry."

Nancy works at Ridge Park School, a public charter school run by National Heritage Academies in the southeast corner of Grand Rapids. The school's approximately 650 students largely live nearby in "Section 8" housing, a government program whereby people in low-income households receive vouchers to help pay their rent. Also included in the school's population are many refugees who have recently settled in Grand Rapids.

In her related role as Ridge Park's homeless liaison, Nancy knows the school families work with very limited food budgets. "Even with food stamps," Nancy says, "they run out of money. Parents were coming to me asking, 'Is there any funding out there for food? Is there anything the school can do to help?' "

Homeless, hungry kids in this suburban location? "They are not living on the streets," says Nancy, "but federal laws have expanded the definition of 'homeless' to include people who live in shelters and those who live with extended family or friends. We have families whose children attended Ridge Park prior to losing their home, and may now live in a downtown shelter. It's our responsibility to provide transportation for them to school." The older students receive free tickets to ride the city bus while Nancy has pieced together a network of drivers for the younger ones.

Familiar with Kids' Food Basket, Nancy requested that her school be put on the waiting list. As more funding was received to serve more schools, Ridge Park worked its way to the top of the list.

As social worker, Nancy generates the list of students who receive the meals. Permission slips are sent home to make sure parents are agreeable. "Many cultures are represented at our school," says Nancy, "so for dietary reasons, we need parent permission."

Sack suppers are distributed at end of day. Some eat the food on the way home. Many students attend an after-school tutoring program called "Homework Club," and eat part or all of their meal there.

Nancy says, "I used to drive a family of four girls home from school who had just moved into permanent housing. On the days the sacks contained a sandwich with cheese, the excited chatter in the car was, 'Mom can make grilled cheese tonight.' "

Parents are very appreciative of the nutritional value of the Sack Suppers. "One refugee mother had never seen a cherry tomato before and brought it in to ask me what it was," says Nancy. "She wanted to make sure her daughter wasn't eating candy."

Nancy has compiled data to verify if the meals have made a difference in any measurable way. Sure enough, attendance has improved as well as test scores. Using a standardized test called the Northwestern Evaluation Association, students who received Sack Suppers grew in competencies an average of 145%, compared to an expected growth of 100% for the time period. "This is numerical proof," says Nancy, "that a regular regimen of nutrition positively impacts student learning."

Anecdotal comments from teachers include that students are sleeping better at night, exhibit better concentration, report a greater sense of self-esteem, and are better equipped to handle the stress of everyday life (family relationships, jobs or lack of jobs, homelessness). They also affirm the Sack Suppers teach families what good nutrition looks like.

Students frequently stop by Nancy's office to inquire when the meals are arriving and she hears testimonials such as this from second grader, Jaden: "It [a Sack Supper] helps me because my granny doesn't always have much food and it keeps me from being sloppy. When I'm hungry, I just keep walking around the house." And, from ten-year-old Montserrat, "My mom drops me off at home after school and goes to work. There's never any food. I eat my Sack Supper while I do my homework."

"It's important to level the playing field for students who live in poverty," says Nancy, "and Kids' Food Basket has made a huge dent in childhood hunger in our school. The students are getting a better education because Sack Suppers take some of the worry out of basic human needs, like a full stomach. I see students and parents begin to trust and value education again. Their thinking is: 'My child is fed, so we can focus on homework and school skills.' "

Srinivas K. Janardan, M.D.
Volunteer

The father of three young daughters living a life full of advantages, Srinivas "Vas" Janardan sought an opportunity to broaden their perspectives. Specifically, he wanted the girls to see how a significant number of people live at the opposite end of the economic spectrum. It didn't take Vas long to discover that volunteer options for teens were limited. Many youngsters were able to find meaningful experiences through their places of worship, but as Hindus without a local temple at the time, that route was closed to the Janardans. Through work colleague Patti Decker, Vas learned of Kids' Food Basket and their need for volunteers of all ages.

"I brought my daughters to Kids' Food Basket one evening a week to assemble Sack Suppers," says Vas. "After six months or so, Patti, who was on the Board of Directors at the time and also led the Community Outreach Committee, asked me to join the board. By then I was committed to the mission and gladly accepted the position."

From 2007-2012, Vas and his fellow board members oversaw tremendous growth. The operation moved from Monroe Street to Butterworth Avenue as funding became available and more space was needed to increase the number of sack meals from 1000 to 1500. "That was a milestone for us," remembers Vas. "Bridget Clark Whitney (Director), Mary K. Hoodhood (founder) and the rest of the staff constantly promoted the cause," says Vas. "With increased community awareness we were able to boost the number of Sack Suppers by 50%."

Then the nonprofit made strides in another area. Jay Ertl, a vice president at Amway Corporation and current Kids' Food Basket Board President, gathered a team of Amway experts to evaluate the ways the organization was completing various tasks with the company's "LEAN" efficiency model. After the study, they were able to better utilize Kids' Food Basket's resources to make more Sacks Suppers in a limited space. "That concept was foreign to Kids' Food Basket as a volunteer organization," says Vas. "Bringing Amway's professional manufacturing practices to the process of making Sack Suppers was revolutionary for us."

"The Amway volunteer team provided suggestions that made huge differences," Vas continues. "They reorganized our work flow, our refrigerator space and the way we stored food. In effect, they built a bridge between manufacturing and a volunteer endeavor, to great success."

In addition to providing the new production process, Amway also built efficient work surfaces for Kids' Food Basket. "With the new procedures in place, we realized we could increase our output to 5000 or even 6000 Sack Suppers a day," says Vas. Accordingly, Kids' Food Basket moved to a larger location on Oak Industrial Drive.

Vas (standing, fourth from left) with fellow Kids' Food Basket board members. Founder Mary K. Hoodhood is seated in the middle and Executive Director Bridget Clark Whitney is seated on the right.

Vas remains active with Kids' Food Basket as a member of the Finance Committee. As a physician, he also brings his knowledge and counsel to the current Nourish Challenge campaign. Until recently the goal was to hit a calorie count for each Sack Supper. "Now we're taking it to the next level by focusing on the nutritional value of each item in the sack," says Vas. "Is each providing long-term growth for the kids? We have struggled to add more fruits and vegetables, as those are the most expensive calories to buy. Our Nourish Challenge campaign aims to raise additional funds to include fruits and vegetables on a daily basis."

Vas feels he's received more than he's given from his association with Kids' Food Basket. "We all get stuck in ruts," he says. "For me, I mostly knew people in the medical community and my religious community. Through Kids' Food Basket I've met people from a wide range of fields and backgrounds that I would not have otherwise met. It's rubbed off on my children, who are now in their early 20s. They have seen that everyone doesn't live as well as they do."

Kids' Food Basket has raised Vas's awareness that it's easy to be blind to those around us. He says, "With so many positive things happening to make Grand Rapids a wonderful place to live, it's easy to forget there's an underprivileged segment of our community not too far away. There are people struggling to survive, hidden in corners, sometimes out of sight. Kids' Food Basket has brought the issue of childhood hunger to the forefront by building awareness that some people need help."

Steve and Lou Anne Davis
Volunteers

Steve Davis was a board member of Indian Trails Camp when Mary K. Hoodhood also came onto that board. He knew nothing about Mary K. or her cause, Kids' Food Basket, he just saw a woman in a wheelchair and thought, "What can *she* do?" Pretty soon he knew the answer to his own question: "A whole lot more than most people." Steve enjoys telling this story on himself, of how his expectations were quickly shattered.

They got to be friends, and about ten years ago Mary K. asked Steve to become a member of the Kids' Food Basket Fund Development Committee. Steve says, "I told her I don't know people with deep pockets, but she still wanted me, so I joined. There were 12 or 15 people at my first meeting and I didn't know anyone except Mary K. They introduced themselves, and by the time it was my turn, I was totally impressed with the quality of the people and their commitment to the mission."

Two years later, Mary K. enlisted Steve and his wife Lou Anne to take on a new position, that of facilitators. In that capacity, the couple supervises a shift of volunteers the first Thursday evening of every month. Most have volunteered longer than the Davises, and hail from Thornapple Community Church, Comerica Bank, Trinitas Classic School and Neland Avenue Christian Reformed Church. During their two-hour stint, about forty people produce 2800 sandwiches, pack 1500 Sack Suppers and repack countless baggies of carrots, cherry tomatoes, crackers and party mix.

Lou Anne is impressed with the level of efficiency at Kids' Food Basket. "In the past I have volunteered at places where no one knows what they're supposed to do," she says. "I never feel like that at Kids' Food Basket. We have a purpose and a goal and know the work we do is vital to feeding hungry kids. We accomplish so much in a short time because the production component is so organized. The whole experience energizes me."

Steve and Lou Anne are touched and motivated by a story Executive Director Bridget Clark Whitney tells of a student who took her Sack Supper home, ate half, and returned to school the next day with the other half. "Didn't you like your Sack Supper?" her teacher asked. "Yes," said the little girl, "but I thought I'd be hungry after school again today." The Davis's grandson just turned eight years old, and Lou Anne gets teary-eyed, thinking one of those hungry children could easily be their grandson. "It makes it all the more real for us," says Lou Anne.

After eight years of service on the Fund Development Committee, Steve is now a Kids' Food Basket Ambassador. As such, he seeks to spread the word wherever he goes and speaks to various groups about the organization. "I wear my Kids' Food Basket hat all the time," says Steve, "and people frequently ask me about it. I tell them about feeding hungry kids until they wish they hadn't asked me," he jokes.

In addition to their volunteer hours, Steve and Lou Anne support Kids' Food Basket by participating in Feast for Kids, the annual spring fundraiser at which local chefs prepare a gourmet dinner and a silent auction is held. Steve has also served at ice cream socials held at various parks and schools during the summer months. Steve convinced his brother Stan to use his van to deliver Sack Suppers to schools.

Lou Anne was instrumental in getting many of her co-workers at The Bank of Holland to volunteer and was also on their sack-producing team for quite a few years. Her service was recognized by the bank when she received the 2008 CARE (Commitment, Action, Responsibility, and Empathy) Award. "I had an audience of 200 people as I made my thank-you speech," says Lou Anne, "and used that opportunity to talk about Kids' Food Basket." Consequently, more bank employees signed on as volunteers.

Mary K. is a constant inspiration to both Steve and Lou Anne. "We do it because she asks," says Steve. And Lou Anne adds, "There are times, after a long day at work, when I'm tired and just want to go home. Then I think about Mary K. and all she accomplishes from a wheelchair. I think 'If she can do so much to help kids despite that handicap, I can certainly make sandwiches for two hours.' "

The Davises have met "some of the most amazing, wonderful people who we now call friends," says Steve. "They all work with smiles on their faces. We can't feed every hungry child, but we're making a big difference. I hope someday we're put out of business."

AliciaMarie Belchak
Mother

AliciaMarie Belchak and her husband Matthew Milzarski suffered from the economic recession of 2008, both losing their jobs. "We went for two months with zero income in our home, not even unemployment benefits. Luckily, we had savings to live on for a while," says AliciaMarie. "We were careful before, but we became even more frugal afterwards. The experience really changed us and gave us a whole new view of life and survival. We still haven't completely rebounded."

Along with their two children, Marie, 9, and Liam, 4, AliciaMarie portrays her family as one with middle class education and thinking, but lower class income. "We're 'gap' people," she says. "We don't qualify for assistance, and we're living on a tight budget just above the line for help. Plus, we pay a mortgage on our home and still have college loans we're paying off. We don't have health insurance benefits through an employer, which means additional bills and sometimes unpaid time off."

Now, juggling part-time jobs, the couple works hard to make the schedule work each week. Matthew is a computer and phone IT technician as well as stay-at-home dad, while AliciaMarie is a freelance writer and a communications specialist for the Grand Rapids Area Chamber of Commerce. As such, it's tough to make ends meet, so the Sack Suppers that Marie and Liam receive at school each day are a blessing. Their typical routine is to pick the children up after school, drive home, help them change their clothes and get washed up, then eat their Sack Suppers. "We always admire the decorations on the bags," says AliciaMarie, referring to the pictures and designs other children draw on the bags to express their love and solidarity. "Sometimes, if they're especially nice, we cut them out and hang them up. Then, Marie and Liam dig in."

AliciaMarie sees a marked improvement in Marie and Liam's attitudes and behavior when they eat those extra calories each day. "They're kinder to one another, and have more energy and stamina," she says. "They can be cranky when they don't get their Sack Suppers. It helps keep them happy and healthy."

Because AliciaMarie believes so strongly in Kids' Food Basket, she gives back through volunteering her time. "There's lots of ways to be involved," she says, "and they don't all involve money, although that's also necessary." As a member of the Outreach Committee, she acts as an ambassador for Kids' Food Basket wherever she goes. "Marie is also a great little ambassador," says AliciaMarie of her daughter. "She is so proud that Kids' Food Basket started at Sibley Elementary, her school. She loves the book *The Girl in the Yellow Dress*, a children's book written to tell the story of the organization's founding."

Marie is now in fourth grade, and AliciaMarie started a Girl Scout troop for Marie and her classmates at Sibley last spring. "We're going to Kids' Food Basket this fall to help pack Sack Suppers," says AliciaMarie. "Most of the kids don't know where the food comes from, so our Girl Scouts will take the message back to the school. A few years ago an older scout in Grand Rapids developed a Kids' Food Basket badge that the girls can earn. I plan to encourage my troop members to pursue that badge."

Through her further involvement in the Kids Helping Kids program, AliciaMarie and her family promoted the 'Go Orange for Hunger' campaign, held in March 2014. The family made YouTube videos about Kids' Food Basket starring the kids as well as signs and chants to share from the sidelines of the St. Patrick's Day Parade. Orange is the national color of hunger awareness, and all over the country people work to spread the word that one in four kids goes hungry every day. AliciaMarie additionally used her expertise in social media to let people know about the 'Go Orange' campaign, and one of her friends took it to his workplace where 30 more people became involved. She also took the promotion to the Chamber of Commerce, where she promoted the event through its social media and staff flyers.

AliciaMarie sees a genuine need in the community for Kids' Food Basket. "So many kids have unstable home lives. Proper nutrition is an important way to help those children."

"It's a time saver, a money saver and a life saver," says AliciaMarie. "We are super appreciative of Kids' Food Basket and Sack Suppers."

AliciaMarie and her family, dressed in their tee shirts for 'Go Orange for Hunger' Day

Mission: *United Church Outreach Ministry values individuals and builds community in southwestern Kent County by providing material and educational assistance to meet basic needs, improve quality of life and promote self-sufficiency.*

UCOM's Mobile Food Truck serves neighbors the first Saturday of each month.

1311 Chicago Drive SW
Wyoming, MI 49509
616.241.4006
ucomgr.org

– United Church Outreach Ministry –

Roots

United Church Outreach Ministry (UCOM) is a stone's throw from Roosevelt Park, an area that has always been a hub for immigrants. In the late 1800s Dutch immigrants built schools and churches and opened grocery stores, bakeries and clothing stores. In the 1960s Latinos began to settle with hopes for a better life. Many came from the fields and orchards of Texas and found similar work in area farms and greenhouses.

In 1969 the women of Smith Memorial Congregational United Church of Christ in Grand Rapids responded to a community need by collecting food and serving hot lunch at Hall Street Elementary School (now Cesar E. Chavez Elementary School). Students marched across Hall Street to the church in shifts until all bellies were filled. Parents came to the church for leftovers to feed their children who were not yet in school. This led to the birth of a food pantry in the church basement. What began as a clothing closet in the parsonage turned into Unity House, a clothing pantry operated from a separate building. These pantries continued for over 20 years.

The church's population dwindled over time; when it was apparent that it could no longer meet the neighborhood's needs, Betsy Dole and other community leaders conducted a feasibility study to form a covenant ministry with the Grand Rapids Association United Church of Christ, and United Church Outreach Ministry (UCOM) was incorporated in 1985.

A Focus on Education

Both Betsy Dole and Jan Williams, UCOM's first Director, believed that, while furnishing food and clothing to people would get them by, only education would get them ahead. In 1985 the Grand Rapids Public Schools mandated homework for all students, but since English was not spoken in many neighborhood homes, Latino children had a distinct disadvantage. Betsy and her colleagues recruited droves of people, primarily retirees, to offer one-to-one tutoring to students after school, and *Homework House* was formed in 1985. Jan developed cutting edge curriculum for this literacy-based program, which focused on reading and math skills and offered enrichment activities and field trips. A six-week course was also offered in the summer.

Expanded Programs and Continued Growth

In 1990 All County Churches Emergency Services System (ACCESS, now called Access of West Michigan) centralized church food pantries, dividing the greater Grand Rapids area into nine geographical areas. Each district chose one Key Food Pantry with the rest designated as support pantries. UCOM became the Key Pantry for southwest Grand Rapids, Wyoming and Grandville.

Jan continued as Director for 16 years with a constant eye on educational and social services. In the early 2000s she and current UCOM Program Director Shawn Keener strengthened the summer school program with many new experiences for the children, including professional art instruction, theater visits and exploration of local gypsum mines. Before Jan retired in 2004, UCOM's Board hired Bruce Roller as Executive Director to lead the expanding agency. With Bruce at the helm, UCOM delved into more areas of service. "The beginnings of many of these programs were serendipitous," says Bruce. "If needs expressed by community members fit in with our mission, we did what we could to find resources that would allow us to provide for those needs."

As programs expanded, UCOM outgrew the church basement, and in 2006 the Matthysse Kuiper DeGraaf Funeral Home sold their Wyoming location to the agency for an affordable sum. No longer was UCOM simply a church ministry; it had developed into a bona fide community resource center.

Programs and Services

UCOM cares about the whole person; as well as supplying material needs, programs are in place to enhance education, improve health and well being, strengthen financial literacy and find jobs.

Youth Education: UCOM's flagship program *Homework House* is still going strong. Dynamic curriculum is updated to meet ongoing educational developments. Under the leadership of UCOM's Education Director, volunteers from Calvin College and other learning institutions provide after-school homework assistance and provide literacy skills and math instruction to students in Cesar Chavez Elementary, Godfrey Elementary and the Early Childhood Learning Center in grades K-5.

The *Believe 2 Become Summer Learning Academy*, offered since 2011 for grades 1-5, focuses on literacy and reading comprehension. Students engage in science, math, art, music, and social studies activities. A field trip to a local attraction that fits the week's theme is a high point for up to 35 students.

Food and Clothing Support: Committed to personal empowerment, UCOM's *Client Choice* pantry is open Tuesday through Friday. Residents in the UCOM service area may shop once a month for a three-day emergency supply of healthy food.

The *Nutritional Options for Wellness (NOW)* pantry is a collaborative effort between UCOM, Spectrum Health and Access of West Michigan. Low-income Kent County clients with chronic illnesses shop weekly for fresh fruits and vegetables, whole grains and low-fat, low-sugar and low-sodium foods. Clients are required to attend six hours of nutrition classes a year, taught by Michigan State University and Spectrum Health educators. In addition, *Cooking Matters* classes at UCOM are taught by YMCA instructors.

Participants in the *Commodity Supplemental Food Program (CSFP)* receive a monthly pre-packed box containing healthy items from each food group. *CSFP* is administered by ACSET and is available for eligible low-income senior citizens. Volunteers, staff and food pantry clients work side by side the first Saturday of each month to serve neighbors in need from the *Mobile Food Truck.* For many families, the monthly mobile food truck is their only exposure to the pantry network.

Gently used clothing is available in UCOM's *Clothing Pantry.* UCOM also accepts furniture donations. If clients have a need for a piece of furniture or an appliance, they can earn it by either volunteering a prescribed number of hours or attending financial classes.

Open Door Press: UCOM has published children's books that offer hope in the face of challenges, available at the UCOM online store and Amazon.com. Another book is scheduled to be published in the fall of 2015.

Health and Social Services: When clients expressed medical concerns five years ago, UCOM and the Calvin College nursing program partnered to provide free health screening. Free blood-pressure checks and blood sugar testing are also provided periodically throughout the year.

The Association for the Blind and Visually Impaired provides free eye exams to screen for glaucoma and impaired vision. UCOM makes dental and medical referrals to Spectrum's Core Health Diabetes Program and other community clinics. Diabetic supplies are available to clients; requests for walkers, canes, wheelchairs and other equipment are directed to support pantries.

Molina Healthcare representatives help clients find affordable health services and assist them in signing up for Medicare and Medicaid. Blue Cross Blue Shield (BCBS) provides supplemental funding to support UCOM's health initiatives and assists clients in signing up for Affordable Health Care

Act insurance. BCBS representatives also assist donors in signing up for Access' Holiday Giving Network program, which supplies Thanksgiving and Christmas dinners to low-income families.

UCOM interns and volunteers help clients apply for Department of Human Services (DHS) bundled benefits online at UCOM's facilities. Benefits for which clients may qualify include food stamps, State Emergency Relief funds and childcare.

The Humane Society partners with UCOM to provide periodic pet clinics, where neighbors bring in their dogs, cats and other pets for free checkups and immunizations.

Financial Services and Work Skills Training: English and Spanish-speaking participants take *Financial Skills Instruction* classes to learn about community resources, budgeting techniques and banking services. Representatives from area banks respond to students' questions at the culminating session. United Way also supports this vital skill-building educational program.

UCOM offers *Volunteer Income Tax Assistance (VITA)* in collaboration with the Kent County Tax Credit Coalition to community members who are at or below 150% of the poverty level. UCOM clients and volunteers benefit from the *Work Skills Training* program while volunteering at UCOM. Participants receive instruction in communication, conflict resolution, interviewing techniques and skills training.

A 2007 Department of Labor grant allowed UCOM to help ex-offenders find jobs. This program has been expanded to assist a diverse cross section of people, including individuals with language barriers and disabilities, find and retain entry-level jobs.

Growing Green Neighbors: Since 2011 the *Square Foot Gardening* program has helped neighbors become more self-sustaining. Participants are given soil, seeds, a raised garden and 16 crops of their choosing. Master gardeners and farmers teach growing tips and answer questions at monthly meetings. As a condition of enrollment, gardeners teach skills

to friends, who then receive their own garden box the following summer.

UCOM's on-site hoop house contains raised gardens, tended by volunteers from organizations such as MOKA (individuals with disabilities from Muskegon, Ottawa, Kent, and Allegan counties). Metro Health and the City of Wyoming partner with UCOM to sponsor a community garden in Marquette Park. Through the *Project Fresh* program, operated by Senior Meals on Wheels and made possible through Senior Millage, participants aged 60+ learn nutrition lessons from MSU extension instructors; they redeem coupons at local farmers markets for fresh produce.

Funding

From its beginning UCOM has been supported through private donations from 50 local churches and hundreds of donors; funding also comes from United Way, foundations and corporations.

Since 2003 the *Friends of UCOM* benefit concert has been an annual highlight. Other fundraisers include a bowling party and the *You R UCOM* luncheon, held at the L.V. Eberhard Center at Grand Valley State University. Mika Meyers Beckett & Jones, Molina Healthcare, Mercantile Bank and other community partners provide sponsorship for these events.

Leadership and Volunteers

UCOM employs eleven staff members including an executive director, a program director and program coordinators, and is led by a 13-member volunteer board.

Tutoring for *Homework House*, stocking shelves and coolers, preparing crafts for the carnival and cleaning the premises are all accomplished by volunteers. Residents from local adult foster homes sort clothing and become involved in pantry operations according to their skill sets and interests. UCOM provides meaningful opportunities to individuals with mobility and cognitive disabilities. People working with Hope Network and Kent Vocational Options (KVO) serve the community by volunteering at UCOM. Individuals doing community service through the courts are also an important part of UCOM's volunteer and workforce development base.

UCOM hosts mission groups from across the United States. Young people tutor and conduct art projects with children and assist with gardening/landscaping, maintenance projects, stocking pantries, personal shopping and office duties. Interns from Jubilee Jobs, the Hispanic Center of West Michigan and Project Cool gain valuable experience throughout the summer. Grand Valley State University Social Work students benefit and contribute by participating in internships at UCOM.

Vision

Similar to Martin Luther King Jr.'s goal, UCOM's vision is one of a beloved community where all people feel loved, valued, honored and respected. UCOM is committed to respond to the changing needs of the community, and its history reflects its pledge to help neighbors help themselves.

Rachel DeMaagd
Client, Volunteer

In 2011 Executive Director Bruce Roller invited a group of individuals with disabilities to UCOM and asked them, "How would you like to be treated when you volunteer at UCOM?"

One of the young women present, Rachel DeMaagd, answered, "We want to be treated like everybody else."

UCOM recently received a five-year grant to expand volunteer opportunities and provide stipends to individuals with disabilities. "Rachel's first words to us became our mantra as we developed this program," says Bruce.

Rachel is the oldest of three sisters, born in Korea. When Rachel was eight years old, the girls were adopted by the DeMaagd family of Grand Rapids. In 2000, after she turned 18, Rachel moved into a group home. She soon realized she needed something different. "I felt like the walls were closing in on me because I had no freedom," says Rachel. "I was told when to wake up, when to eat and when I could go out. My attitude was bad and I tried to run away. I didn't care for myself and didn't want to accept help." Over the next 11 years Rachel lived in six different group homes.

With determination and hard work, Rachel's life began to change. In 2008 she opened "Rachel's Little Coffee Shop" through Hope Network's Micro-Enterprise Program and gained confidence as she made business decisions. ARC Kent County, an advocacy organization for individuals with disabilities, helped Rachel explore alternative living arrangements. Attending the meeting at UCOM opened even more doors for her.

Rachel immediately endeared herself to UCOM staff as she volunteered, according to Bruce. "Rachel became a wonderful receptionist," he says. "She loves children, and there were always five or six children gathered around her desk, coloring or drawing. At the same time she answered phones and paged people, always with a 'big smile in her voice'."

UCOM's approach to involving people with disabilities is to provide meaningful opportunities based on their strengths and goals, rather than on the disability or barrier. "When we identify what people can and want to do, then we can lead them to training programs that make those goals possible," says Bruce. "When we got to know Rachel we discovered that she is empathetic and nonjudgmental. She is a compelling public speaker, and she has a passion for 'freeing,' as she sees it, individuals with disabilities from group homes."

Rachel completed training as a Local Leader through Partners For Freedom, which is funded by Michigan Developmental Disabilities Council through Arc Michigan. In this role she offers hope to others as she counsels peers and speaks across Michigan about how self-determination changed her life. She has made presentations about what she has gained through her relationship with UCOM at Park Church, Plymouth United Church of Christ and the 2013 *You R UCOM* luncheon at the L.V. Eberhard Center of Grand Valley State University. "In front of 200 people," says Rachel, "I said UCOM was more than a food pantry; they share food and they also share their smiles. They care about everyone who walks through their doors."

In 2011 Rachel's hope of living independently became a reality. "My friends from UCOM helped me move into my new apartment," says Rachel. "I couldn't have done it without them. Being in my own place is like a dream. I can go out with friends and take walks when I want to. I needed that little taste of freedom. It's like kicking off my shoes on the beach and running in the sand."

Community Living Support staff members, hired by Rachel though Medicaid funding, help with food preparation and provide transportation. Rachel knows that responsibility comes with privilege; she cleans her apartment, keeps a schedule and budget on her computer and pays her staff.

Rachel continues to inspire people. She recently spoke about her experiences to a diverse audience of lawmakers and individuals with disabilities at a Michigan Developmental Disabilities Council conference. She has been contracted as a counselor at a local camp where she will speak with young women with disabilities. Small steps have led to victories for Rachel. UCOM community members initially helped her navigate the Grand Rapids transit system, and today she can utilize her GO!Bus pass to ride the bus herself. Rachel signed up for the UCOM bowling fundraiser and raised $100 to give back to this organization that has embraced her. She has attended church with UCOM staff members, which allows her to further expand her support network and build relationships.

When people with disabilities are segregated into costly programs, growth is hampered and creativity is squelched. When they are engaged in a loving community and form authentic relationships, they contribute to a greater purpose and the need for paid services diminishes. UCOM has provided Rachel with that sense of community. "The people at UCOM are good listeners and they laugh at all my jokes, even the ones that aren't funny," says Rachel. "They have good hearts, and they are like my family."

Jawaun Kenney
UCOM Operations Manager and Volunteer Advocate

Jawaun Kenney wears many hats at UCOM. Although his official titles are Operations Manager and Volunteer Advocate, he is also a gardener, food pantry shelf stocker, mechanic to a fleet of vehicles, and the go-to guy when anything needs to be picked up, delivered, or constructed. Affable and good-humored, Jawaun is often the first face that UCOM volunteers see whether they are from a church, an out-of-town mission group or a court-mandated Community Service group. "Our short-term goal is to feed as many people as possible," says Jawaun. "The pantry moves a thousand miles a minute, and the volunteers get the product out quickly.

"I think UCOM volunteers get a different outlook on the face of hunger," he continues. "People don't always look the part. A lot of people judge someone based on their clothes or their car. They don't understand that maybe it was a bad week or month; maybe they have cancer and are putting all their money toward medical bills. They see the exterior but don't see all the pressures a person is facing. It's easy to play Monday morning quarterback, but when they get involved, volunteers see that it could be their brother, sister or mother needing a helping hand some day."

No stranger himself to challenges, Jawaun describes his childhood struggles as a "helpful experience." Jawaun and his twin brother were raised by their mother and grandmother in Detroit. "It's important for kids to keep busy," says Jawaun, "and we didn't have many opportunities. The Boys & Girls Club in our area served hundreds of kids. I'm thankful I at least had football to keep me focused."

Jawaun went to college on an athletic scholarship but did not graduate. "There I was, 24 years old and lost," he says. "I came to Grand Rapids in 2007 with a duffel bag and found a job with a cable company." Then Jawaun decided to pursue a degree in criminal justice because he wanted to help people who faced similar challenges. Because part of his focus was community service workers, he was assigned to UCOM through a work-study program. When this assignment ended he continued to volunteer, and UCOM offered him a job in 2010.

Jawaun has passed on lessons he's learned at UCOM to his fiancé Katie's four boys: Anthony (16), Alex (13), Rueben (12) and Jordan (10). "We try to protect the boys from the drugs and crime that I saw growing up," he says. The boys are involved in football at the Siedman Center Boys & Girls Club, where Jawaun has coached for several years. "I tell my players something I've learned at UCOM," says Jawaun. "If you practice something it becomes a habit, and once it becomes a habit it creates character. Character is built in community. It's amazing to see when that happens. People come back to UCOM after they get their feet back on the ground. Pretty soon they're the ones dropping off food and clothing donations."

Jawaun and Katie's boys have taken part in UCOM's Homework House program and the *Believe 2 Become* Summer Learning Academy. "Education is the most important thing," says Jawaun. "Not only have the boys improved academically, they've grown socially. This is a safe place and a diverse group. Nobody is judged. Our kids also volunteer for events like UCOM's carnival, and on lazy summer days I tell them, 'Come on, let's move some furniture!' "

When UCOM began the Square Foot Gardening program, Jawaun took part in the design and construction of the 4' x 4' raised boxes. He also signed his family up to participate. "It's a teaching tool," he says. "The boys know that things don't grow unless they take time to water and weed. Local groceries don't have a huge selection, and produce can be expensive, but I can buy a packet of tomato seeds for $1.00 and harvest 80 tomatoes, and that's spaghetti sauce for a few months. The reaction I get when I deliver the garden boxes to an elderly lady is priceless. She's so grateful that she offers me her last dollar, but I say 'Your smile is enough.' When I was little I watched my grandma shovel snow and rake leaves, and nobody was there to help her. When I do that for others, it makes me feel fulfilled.

Jawaun Kenney, pictured with faithful
UCOM volunteers

"I think its tough for people in this neighborhood to get help because of fear over immigration issues," Jawaun continues. "But at UCOM, even if people don't have the 'right' identification, we still help. We care about the whole person. We help with material things and help people find jobs, and so many clients give back. On *Mobile Food Pantry* days, clients work side-by-side with staff. I love when moms send their kids to help during the week. At UCOM I've learned about selflessness. For events and projects, we come in like a swarm of bees to get it done. We see the community interacting and having the time of their lives in a safe environment. We feel their appreciation, and that's the biggest reward."

Maria and Gaby Favela
Clients, Volunteers

Maria Favela and her three-year-old daughter Gaby moved from Chicago to the heart of Grand Rapids' Hispanic district in 1997 to seek a safer, better life.

"When you move to a new city," recalls Maria, "it can be difficult getting established. We ran into a bit of a hiccup and someone told me about an organization down the street that would give us food. Coming from a dog-eat-dog city like Chicago, this was a new concept for me. *An organization that gives away food? What do they want in return?* I went to UCOM, and I remember feeling so embarrassed to be in the position to ask for food, but Jan Williams, the Executive Director at the time, and (UCOM Emergency Services Director) Diana DeYoung were such kind ladies; they made me feel like it was okay. After I showed our identification and answered a few questions, they gave me food. Still, I kept thinking *What else do they want?*"

In time Maria became convinced that no strings were attached, and she had a desire to give back. Since UCOM's clientele was primarily Hispanic, a communication gap often existed between staff and food pantry clients. When Maria was asked to help with translating she eagerly accepted the opportunity.

"Since I worked third shift full time, I could only volunteer one day a week, and that day was Wednesday," says Maria. The Hispanic community knew that, and they would make it a point to come on Wednesdays." Since the need for translating services was so deep, UCOM applied for a grant and Maria was paid for her work. Because of this opportunity, along with fierce determination and hard work, she transitioned from client to servant.

Over the years Maria has lent her time and talents to cater authentic Mexican food for annual fiesta-themed Friends of UCOM benefit concerts. For other events she is involved in setup, cleanup and everything in between. Volunteering at the food pantry has always been Maria's mission, and her work inspired her daughter Gaby to become involved at an early age.

"I remember the first time I came to UCOM when I was in second grade," says Gaby. "My mom picked me up from school on a rainy day and brought me to UCOM. I was so impressed by how they were helping people, and I was proud of my mom's work."

Through the years Gaby found ways that she, too, could serve. During summer vacations she stocked shelves, packed boxes and helped people shop at the pantry. She attended Homework House after elementary school, and as a high school student she tutored students who attended the program.

As Gaby grew older she learned valuable skills as the UCOM office assistant. "Being at UCOM gave me a passion for being a part of this community," she says, "and they have done so much for me." Gaby received a scholarship through a UCOM connection to receive music lessons and join the St. Cecelia Youth Choir during her high school years.

Now a junior at Hope College, Gaby represents the first generation in the Favela family to attend a university. She plans to major in social work and hopes to work with the Michigan migrant community.

"When I was in seventh grade," she recalls, "there was a fire at a Greenville orchard and migrant families were displaced. (UCOM Executive Director) Bruce Roller rented a U-Haul and loaded it with clothes, furniture and food. He asked my mom to join him to translate, and I went along as well. I met kids my own age who worked in the fields alongside their parents, but even though they had a very difficult life they were joyful; they cooked food for us on hotplates and were servants to us. I realized that people aren't defined by their circumstances."

The Favelas have experienced and witnessed the challenges faced by people who come to the United States to improve their circumstances. Maria's father came from Mexico in the 1950s as a 17-year-old migrant worker and earned his citizenship through the *Bracero Program*, an initiative between the United States and Mexico from 1942-1964 that offered the possibility of legal status to farm workers. His sacrifices opened doors for other family members, many of whom have served in the U.S. military and become public servants. But Maria remembers how difficult life was for her mother, who did not speak English and remained isolated in her new country.

"I don't remember anyone reaching out to help my mom," says Maria. "If she'd had a place like UCOM, it would have made a world of difference. By being a part of UCOM, I can be a voice for my people. There might be language barriers at other pantries, but people feel safe and comfortable here, and there is no judgment.

"At UCOM I encountered people of faith. I had walked away from the church for many years, but I went back and became involved. The way people treated me made me realize there is still good in the world, so I will always have a spot in my heart for UCOM."

Gabriella de la Vega
Client, Volunteer, Board Member

When Gabriella de la Vega immigrated to Grand Rapids from Mexico in 1996 with her three young children, they brought only what they could carry. Seven-year-old Gabriela brought her Cabbage Patch dolls and two-year-old Carla clutched her beloved stuffed horse. Gabriella carried two-month-old José and a small diaper bag. "We had faith," says Gabriella, "and we prayed together that everything would be okay."

Gabriella's mother Maria had come to Michigan several years earlier and was able to share her home with her daughter and grandchildren. "When you come to a new country and do not speak the language," says Gabriella, "it is difficult to start a new life. When you have little children, finding resources for them can be a challenge.

"I called a Spanish-speaking man who worked at a newspaper and he referred me to ACCESS," she continues. "The pantry in my area was UCOM, which was housed in a church at that time. They gave us basic

things, which started us on a path toward improvement. I was so relieved that somebody cared about us. The people at UCOM did not judge us–they were patient and kind, gave us love and hope, and connected us to other agencies. I told myself that one day I would do something to give back to this beautiful community."

Gabriella worked hard to improve her circumstances by taking English classes through the Grand Rapids Public Schools and studying at Grand Rapids Community College. In 1998, along with friends from St. Andrews Parish, she started a television program on WKTV called *A Toda Máquina,* which means "at full speed." The premise of the show was to feature success stories of Hispanic residents and empower them by pointing to organizations that could improve their lives. The program conveyed the message that community makes a difference–something Gabriella had learned firsthand at UCOM. Gabriella's next media job was hosting a radio program in Wyoming, ironically in a building that is adjacent to UCOM's current location on Chicago Drive. In this show as well, the fundamental message was to give hope to Latinos.

"People need to know that someone out there has compassion. When I came to this country, someone–I don't know who, but someone–believed in me enough to give me food and clothing through UCOM, and that made me who I am. These people were angels, giving selflessly."

Connecting with UCOM allowed Gabriella to network with other organizations. When the Red Cross receives emergency calls from Spanish-speaking people, Gabriella serves as interpreter. She volunteers as a translator at the Hispanic Center as well, many times in situations when a family member's safety is at risk. "Everyone has struggles," she says. "I can be mad or sad about my own circumstances, but to help someone else you need to find the strength to be positive and show compassion."

Currently Gabriella hosts a weekend radio program on WYCE in which she combines music with inspirational stories. As a frequent emcee for local Mexican festivals and UCOM events, Gabriella can captivate an audience with her enthusiasm and musicality, but away from a crowd her warmth, compassion and ability to connect with people come through.

"I've had the opportunity to get to know people with many needs as an aide in a nursing home and a hospice facility," she says. "Because of my dark hair and accent, sometimes people would say, 'Don't touch me. I can't understand you.' But I suffered through their pain with them and served them, and after we got to know one another these elderly Polish and Dutch people didn't notice our differences, and they humbly shared their stories with me. If you are a true believer in God you will see others how He sees them, and you will respect them regardless of color or language."

Gabriella recently accepted an invitation to serve on UCOM's board. "I hope I can encourage people who have benefitted from UCOM to give back, because I know it makes life richer and more fulfilling. You never know whose future you'll impact, even when you make what seems like a small contribution."

In 2009 Gabriella married Luis Ramirez, a business owner who has provided financial support to many local organizations. Her family joins her at festivals and events, and her children are following in her footsteps. Gabriela, 25, attended Western Michigan University and is now a compassionate mother herself. Carla, 20, is service-minded and a sophomore at Calvin College, where Gabriella will serve on the Parent Council. José, 18, is a percussionist and composer and attends Grand Rapids Community College.

An entrepreneur in Mexico, Gabriella's mother Maria now owns Connie's Bridal and Alterations, which has become a labor of love for the entire family. "My mom opened a path for us," says Gabriella. "She didn't have a lot of help when she came here, but she is grateful for what UCOM has done for us."

Gabriella reached the milestone of becoming a United States citizen on July 4, 2013. "I love this country," she says. "We left our friends, family, and everything familiar behind, and you don't ever forget where you came from. We are not here to take away, but to make a difference. It's like a circle—organizations like UCOM gave to us when we needed to survive, and now we give back to them. I tell people that we are so blessed in this community. We have *everything* we need, so anything is possible."

Annette Huitron
Volunteer, Client

Annette Huitron's family moved to Grand Rapids from Texas in 1999 because her parents had heard about wonderful opportunities and a thriving Hispanic community in the city. Although her father found a job in Michigan, he worked long hours for little pay, so the "better life" that was desired was not achieved. When the rest of her family returned to Texas, 14-year-old Annette stayed behind. She had to choose between continuing her education and earning money to support herself. It was a matter of survival; she dropped out of school and took on two jobs to make ends meet.

Working long hours without family support took a toll on Annette. She missed connecting with her peers at school, and she felt like she was growing up too fast. "I was lonely, depressed and scared," says Annette. "I knew I had to distract myself and I wanted to keep busy with other things instead of thinking about my problems, so one day I stopped at UCOM, which was just across the street from my home on Hall Street." Making that seemingly spur-of-the-moment decision has had a profound impact on Annette's life and on the lives of countless others.

When she volunteered at the food pantry, Annette immediately sensed that UCOM offered not only food and clothing, but also compassion and safety. Keeping busy and giving to others lifted her depression and motivated her to become more involved at UCOM over the years. Annette's warm, empathetic manner puts UCOM clients at ease as she serves as a translator and answers the phone. She directs food truck deliveries and helps pantry shoppers make healthy choices. She is a frequent volunteer at the Mobile Food Pantry, which serves clients at UCOM grounds on the first Saturday of every month, and she helps where needed at fundraising events.

Annette and her husband José have four children: Victor (8), Desiree (7), Josselyn (5) and Billy (2). When Josselyn was born, Annette quit her job because all her wages were spent on childcare. As the Huitron family grew, UCOM was there to help with baby supplies, diapers and clothing. Today, despite her very busy life, Annette volunteers up to six hours daily at UCOM, often with her kids in tow. "I have explained to my kids that UCOM has helped us a lot," says Annette, "so they want to volunteer with me. UCOM is like our family. I never realized that people could be so good without wanting something from me. The staff gave me hope and love. They showed me the right path and taught me how to be a good mom. I learned a lot of things the hard way, and I want something better for my kids. I know that the people at UCOM are looking out for them."

UCOM has helped many of Annette's acquaintances find jobs. In observing others' employment struggles, she realized that education was the key to opportunity and better jobs and regretted dropping out of high school. But with her husband José's encouragement and coaching, Annette earned her GED in 2010. "It was really hard; some days I felt like quitting," she recalls. "Now my goal is that all of my kids graduate from high school, and I know UCOM cares about their education. In July they'll go to summer school (Believe 2 Become). When school starts, UCOM gives kids backpacks filled with supplies. Last year Victor loved Homework House after school; the staff taught him how to read better, and he met all his goals at school!" This fall, three of Annette's children will attend Homework House.

Photo courtesy of KriZma Photography

As a student in UCOM's cooking classes, Annette learned how to interpret food labels and cook healthy meals for her family. "I teach my kids what I learn," she says, "and when they shop with me they know that if we don't have the money or need the item, we don't buy it." Annette combines her knowledge and skills when she cooks authentic Mexican fare for large church groups that volunteer at UCOM.

UCOM showers its volunteers with appreciative gestures. "When UCOM gets furniture donations," Annette says, "they let volunteers choose what they need. They know it's important to make a house into a home." When the fence around the Huitrons' home fell into disrepair, the Lee Street Christian Reformed Church, one of UCOM's affiliates, sent volunteers to not only fix the fence but also paint the entire house.

The healing that Annette has received at UCOM extends even beyond physical and emotional needs. Being a part of the community has strengthened her faith. After Annette mentioned that she had not been baptized, (Executive Director) Bruce Roller, an ordained minister, made it happen.

Annette credits UCOM for breaking the cycle of poverty in her family, and her story is an example of the abundant reciprocity that is present in UCOM's vibrant and gracious atmosphere. "UCOM has taken away a lot of suffering for so many people, including me," she says. "I can never pay them back but I will always keep trying."

D.A. BLODGETT - ST. JOHN'S
HOMES AND HOPE FOR CHILDREN SINCE 1887

*Mission: Helping children and empowering families
by providing safety, advocacy and support*

Leonard Street Campus:
805 Leonard St. NE
Grand Rapids, MI 49503
616.451.2021

Knapp Street Campus:
2355 Knapp Street NE
Grand Rapids, MI 49505
616.361.5227

dabsj.org

– D.A. Blodgett-St. John's –

Roots

In the 1880s Grand Rapids was a bustling commercial center fueled by the lumber industry. Left out of the city's prosperity, however, was an alarming number of children made homeless as epidemics of typhus, diphtheria, scarlet fever and cholera swept through West Michigan. Malnourished, sick children begged in the streets, and leading citizens banded together to help them. As early as 1882 Bishop Henry Richter exhorted the Catholic community to build an orphanage. With a $60,000 bequest from wealthy lumberman John Clancy in 1884, plans were soon underway.

Meanwhile, Jennie Blodgett and Emily Clark were planning the Children's Aid Society with funds from Jennie's husband, Delos Abiel ("D. A.") Blodgett. In 1887 the Blodgett-Clark project commenced at 42 Lafayette. Before long it would be called the D.A. Blodgett Home for Children.

Up the street, on the corner of Lafayette and Leonard, Bishop Richter's "St. John's Orphan Asylum" was under construction. The four-story building opened in 1889.

St. John's Orphanage/Home from 1889-1960

Over the next thirty years, both ventures expanded to accommodate wave after wave of orphans. In 1908 the Blodgetts built a stately building on Cherry Street, which became the D.A. Blodgett Orphanage; children of all faiths and backgrounds received expert physical care and schooling at the facility. But both the Blodgetts and the Dominican Sisters of St. John's soon realized the limitations of custodial care. The Blodgetts spoke for both agencies when they observed, "[Our children] have everything they need, except a family."

Children at D.A. Blodgett Home for Children, 1922

By the early 1920s, foster programs were established at both agencies. For the rest of the century, advancements in medicine and greater acceptance of foster care and adoption brought an end to traditional orphanages. By 1946, more than 60% of children served by D.A. Blodgett Home for Children and St. John's Home were in foster care.

In the years following World War II, ominous societal changes created difficult new challenges for home placement programs. The modern "orphan" was now likely to be a victim of family violence, abuse and neglect fueled by a rise in alcoholism and drug use. Some children needed much more than a new family could provide.

D.A. Blodgett for Children began offering new prevention services to vulnerable families. Mentoring programs, in particular *Big Brothers Big Sisters*, were added

Twins Donna and Ricky with Sr. Immaculata when St. John's closed, June 1960–Photo Courtesy of MLive Grand Rapids Press

in 1965. Since then, more than a dozen specialized foster and adoption programs and community-based programs have been made available. St. John's Home began focusing exclusively on treating young victims of abuse in its residential program. After St. John's Home's residential program was relocated to a new campus on Knapp Street in 1992, the *KidsFirst* program was founded to provide emergency shelter to abused children in 1998.

A Merger Meant To Be

Over the course of many decades and with common missions, the two agencies began collaborating. A St. John's orphan became a D.A. Blodgett for Children adopted child, and a D.A. Blodgett for Children foster child came to St. John's Home for treatment.

In early 2009, leaders at D.A. Blodgett for Children and St. John's Home began to discuss the merits of a merger. When this unification became official on January 1, 2010, eighteen different programs and services were brought together.

Out of respect for the founding fathers and mothers and thousands of donors and volunteers, the historic names were preserved as the agency was renamed "D.A. Blodgett-St. John's." It is one of Michigan's largest child welfare agencies.

Programs

D.A. Blodgett-St. John's vision is to be the leader in creating a community where all children are treasured and families are strong. The organization works toward this ideal through mentoring, residential care, foster care, emergency shelter, adoption and school and community based counseling programs.

Mentoring comes in many different shapes and forms. Since 1965, D.A. Blodgett-St. John's has served all of Kent County with *Big Brothers Big Sisters*, a nationally recognized mentoring program. Other mentoring programs include the *Amachi Program* for children with a parent incarcerated in a state or federal correctional facility; the *School Based Program* for children who struggle with academic performance, social interactions and self-esteem; and the *Sisters In Support Program* that provides mentoring services to young moms, helping them to cope with parenting, school and financial responsibilities.

D.A. Blodgett-St. John's provides residential treatment in a warm, home-like setting for boys and girls who have suffered abuse and neglect. *The Children's Home* provides therapy for boys and girls from ages six to 12 with an emphasis on preparing them for pre-adoptive homes or to return to rehabilitated families, and *Adolescent Treatment* challenges teens to develop healthy identities and provides attentive preparation for new placements.

While in residential care on a beautiful 25-acre campus within the

City of Grand Rapids, children live in eight-bedroom residential homes. Each home has a comfortable living area, an open kitchen, dining area and large recreation room. Daily therapeutic activities create strong bonds among children and their counselors. Many activities are planned and led by full time Activity Specialists who focus on the performing arts and adventure education.

D.A. Blodgett-St. John's residents attend the Grand Rapids Public Schools or special programs offered by the Kent Intermediate School District. Three full-time educational specialists and four therapists assist students during the school day to help them achieve success in the classroom. A counseling team assists with homework and encourages students to participate in extracurricular activities, including sports, music and club memberships. During the summer, every student attends a ten-week summer school program. Since 1995, D.A. Blodgett-St. John's has offered a free college education to any young person who wants to attend, and so far hundreds have taken advantage of the offer.

When a child is abused or neglected by his or her parent(s) or another family member, *foster parents* are able to provide a loving and safe home until their family situation improves. The goal is for the child and biological parents to be reunited in a timely manner. When this is not possible, *adoption* becomes the goal, and D.A. Blodgett-St. John's has a full range of services available.

About 70% of all children in foster care are at the facility because their parents have a substance abuse problem. Adult substance abuse, mental illness and child sexual abuse contribute to an atmosphere where more and more children need a safe, loving environment while their parents work on treatment.

Since 1998 D.A. Blodgett-St. John's has provided emergency shelter services for Kent County children in two comfortable homes. Called *KidsFirst*, the doors are always open to battered and neglected children and adolescents brought by public safety officers or Protective Services workers.

D.A. Blodgett-St. John's offers many different types of therapy and supportive services; each is designed to help children and parents take steps to a better future. Services include treatment of delinquency in adolescents, assistance for families with a disabled child, parenting education for pregnant women and young parents, community and mental health services and in-school services.

Funding

D.A. Blodgett-St. John's receives funding from a variety of sources including Department of Human Services, Department of Community Health, Family Courts, United Way, private and corporate foundations and thousands of donors throughout the region. The agency also holds a number of special events throughout the year: *Bowl For Kids' Sake, Golf For Kids' Sake, The KidsFirst Open* and the annual *Guild Ball*.

Vision

No one can say what the future holds for D.A. Blodgett-St. John's and the children and families it serves. Who knows what challenges await the most vulnerable members of our community? What we do know is that, for organizations that have stood the test of time, very often "the past is a prologue."

Over the past century and a quarter, D.A. Blodgett-St. John's has provided a caring and humane response to children in need in the West Michigan community.

D.A. Blodgett-St. John's has never wavered from the fundamental belief that the quality of a community is best measured by the way it responds to its most vulnerable members. While the challenges may change for vulnerable children, the spirit of this remarkable agency will not. It will continue to regard its work, as some of its earliest leaders once claimed, as a "privilege to give children we care for a fair chance in life." As D.A. Blodgett-St. John's does this crucial work, it is fueled by its vision of a community where all children are treasured and families are strong.

Linda Hopkins
Donna Newell
Orphans

It was a sad day for sisters Linda and Donna McNamara when they learned they had to split up and leave St. John's Home. The building, a four-story Victorian asylum built 70 years earlier, didn't fit the dwindling orphan demographics of 1959 or the new philosophy of individualization. The remaining children would be placed with adoptive or foster families.

"I wanted to live at St. John's forever," says Donna. "To me it was home, love, safety and structure."

Linda and Donna, along with Donna's twin brother Rick, had come to St. John's after being taken away from their alcoholic, neglectful and abusive parents when Linda was seven years old and the twins barely four. St. John's would be their home and refuge for the next six years.

"I have wonderful memories of St. John's," says Donna. "I loved the structure of our days. We woke to a bell ringing and ate breakfast in the large dining room where we sat at designated tables. There were four dorms lined with beds, one each for the big boys, little boys, big girls and little girls. I remember standing in a long line to have my hair brushed. We kids all wore the same outfits, like uniforms. We attended school at the Home, and later at East and West Leonard schools."

There was lots of fun at the orphanage. Donna remembers walks to nearby parks to play baseball and swim. They visited a farm and played in the barn. The children watched movies in the dining room and roller skated in the cavernous basement. "One April Fools' Day the nuns woke us up and we had cake and ice cream for breakfast," says Donna.

Linda remembers Christmas parties at the country club with gifts from Santa. One Christmas a family invited Linda to their home for the day. "I had such a wonderful time; I thought, 'I wish they would adopt me,' " remembers Linda. She also made a "through-the-fence" friend, a girl from the neighborhood who brought along her doll to pass back and forth.

It's the love and kindness of the Dominican Sisters Linda and Donna most remember. "On my first day at St. John's I was crying and somehow landed in the kitchen," says Linda. "Sr. Leo, the cook, started a conversation with me and said, 'If you ever want cookies, come see me.' We got to be good friends."

For Donna, Sr. Immaculata was a special and caring person. "She was strict, but loving," says Donna. "Every time I came back to St. John's she greeted me with open arms and swung me around."

Throughout those years of 1954-1959, Linda, Donna and Rick went back to live with their parents several times, as the ideal was to have children reunited with their biological parents when possible. "They'd stop drinking for short periods and demand we go back to them," says Linda. "Pretty soon

Mom was boarding up the windows to keep Dad out, but she always let him in eventually."

The three siblings were also in and out of St. John's to various foster homes over the years, but those situations never lasted. On Sundays the kids dressed up to impress couples looking to adopt, "but they all wanted babies," says Linda. Through it all, Linda was like a mother—a nurturer—to her younger brother and sister. "I dressed them, I hugged them, I watched out for them," she says.

Then came the closing of the orphanage and the day the McNamara children were scattered to different foster and adoptive homes in Kentwood, Rockford and Muskegon.

About five years later, Donna made a shopping trip to Atlantic Mills with a girlfriend and her father. "I didn't want to go," remembers Donna. "I was just out of the shower and my hair was wet. Somehow they persuaded me to go despite my hesitation." The sisters believe it was divine intervention. While in the dressing rooms, Donna heard a familiar laugh. When the girl passed by, Donna recognized her profile and found the courage to ask, "Are you Linda?"

Sr. Olga (the girls' second grade teacher at St. John's Home), Linda, Sr. Leo (cook) and Donna

A joyous reunion ensued, with hugs and tears and the quick exchange of phone numbers. When, a short time later, Donna was forbidden by her adoptive mother to contact Linda, she cried for a solid month, and secretly kept Linda's phone number. It was another six years before Donna could use that number to invite Linda, now 22, to her high school graduation. Linda and Donna have been in constant communication ever since and were reunited with their brother Rick Bourdon in the early '70s.

"St. John's Home gave me some good childhood memories to offset many unhappy ones," says Donna. "I am thankful it was a stable environment and a God-centered institution, as that provided me with emotional and spiritual sustenance for what I would later face as a teen."

Linda says, "St. John's was my saving grace. I loved it."

Harold and Jan Woods
Foster Parents

Before they married in 1963, Harold and Jan Woods talked about having lots of children, maybe a dozen or even thirteen, a baker's dozen. Over the next decade-and-a-half they made good progress on their dream, bringing seven children into the world. Then Jan told Harold, "I gave birth to the first half, you're in charge of the rest." Harold said that was no problem—he'd get them "ready-made."

Through her position as a part-time nurse in the pediatric department of St. Mary's Hospital, Jan saw lots of kids with special needs who had been neglected, abused and abandoned by their families. "The first young girl we took in had severe burns from being placed in a bathtub of scalding water as a form of discipline," says Harold. "She was in the hospital for several weeks, needing a salve applied twice a day. It broke Jan's heart. She said, 'I can take her home and treat her there as well as we can in the hospital.' So that's what we did."

In 1970 Harold and Jan became licensed foster parents through D.A. Blodgett Home for Children. The agency's staff was confident they could send special needs kids to the couple, knowing they would receive the nursing care they needed. Thus a steady stream of foster kids was welcomed into their Rockford home.

Jan and Harold adopted seven of the children they fostered, besting the baker's dozen by one. Between their biological, adopted, and foster children, the Woodses had somewhere between three and ten children in their home at all times over the next 41 years. It helped that Jan worked part-time and third shift so she was home to get the kids off to school each morning. Harold's special time with them was when he came home from work at 5:00—supper, family time, bath time, bedtime.

The first foster children Jan and Harold took in were fairly healthy, but as time went on they received more and more fragile children. Alexis was blind and severely brain damaged; she needed a tracheotomy, a feeding tube, a suction machine and oxygen tanks. "I put the tube down her nose every day for seven months until the doctors accepted I was not going to give up," says Jan. "Death is not our call to make. As parents, we fight for our children—we hold them, feed them, love them. We finally found a doctor who would take care of Alexis; it was a lot of work, but it was worth it to see her happy and smiling."

Through it all, a social worker from D.A. Blodgett made monthly visits to the Woods's home. "We were a team, working together in the best interests of each child," says Jan.

Jan became very involved in D.A. Blodgett's Foster Parent Advisory Council, a group of eight or so women who supported each other and supported the agency. They met with Mary Lou Bomgaars, Licensing

Supervisor for foster homes, nurses and social workers to discuss issues germane to their roles, and the women mentored other foster parents. They started a clothing room where foster parents could "shop" for children's apparel. The women also provided welcome, birthday and graduation gifts to the kids.

There have been many changes since Harold and Jan started as foster parents. "Years ago," says Jan, "the system made it difficult for foster parents to adopt the children they were caring for. As time went on, that completely reversed and now foster parents have the first chance to adopt that child."

The level of involvement by foster parents with the court system has also evolved. "In the beginning, we didn't even know the kids' last names," says Jan. "Now you get a report full of pertinent details. We are encouraged to speak up and work as a team to decide the child's future."

Harold and Jan's outstanding service to children has not gone unnoticed. Among their awards are the *Foster Family of the Year* presented in 1993 by the Foster and Adoptive Parent Association, the *Daisy Franks Recruitment Award* in 2003 from D.A. Blodgett, and the *Angels in Adoption Award* from the Congressional Coalition on Adoption Institute in 2006, presented by Congressman Vern Ehlers.

Now in their early 70s and facing health challenges, Harold and Jan have one last adopted child at home, perhaps their greatest challenge. Christopher is a victim of shaken baby syndrome. As such, he is blind, spastic, unable to swallow, unable to move any limbs with purpose, has seizures, and is tube-fed and wheelchair-bound. His life expectancy was only a few years, but with love, hugs and continual care, Christopher is almost 13. "He cannot speak," says Harold, "but Christopher lets his feelings be known. We love him and he loves us."

41 years.

45 foster children.

How did they do it?

"We just love kids," says Jan.

Marshall Booker
Former Counselor and Current Amachi Mentor

Marshall Booker's first job after college in 1987 was with D.A. Blodgett Services for Children and Families as a Case Aide Transporter. "I drove kids to their doctor and social work appointments and for supervised visits with their parents," says Marshall. "Wherever they needed to go, I drove."

As such, he met lots of youngsters. Marshall says, "Kids are wary of newcomers. You can't force it; you just have to be who you are. The most important thing is to let them know you love them and care for them. We developed bonds over time."

The next year Marshall briefly took a position as a part-time counselor at D.A. Blodgett, followed by a full-time position at St. John's Home. From day one, Marshall heeded the advice of supervisor Ray Miller who told him: "You have to start out being tough on the kids, then you can soften up. It won't work if you start out soft, then try to harden up."

"They knew I was tough on them, but they knew I loved them, too," says Marshall. He saw that once the kids got comfortable and knew they were in a safe environment, they did well. He loved to see the growth from when a kid entered the program until he left, six months to two years later— how they grew morally, spiritually and academically.

"D.A. Blodgett-St. John's is one of the best programs in the state," says Marshall. "I attended grad school while I was working as an Educational Coordinator, and one of my placements was with St. John's. I got a firsthand look at the legislative process on trips to Lansing with (Executive Director) David VanRooy. I saw how he championed the kids, how he loved them. It was a great learning process for me."

Marshall remained at St. John's for 11 years as a counselor and Educational Coordinator, then left to work as a social worker for the Grand Rapids Public Schools.

Marshall's world shattered when, on July 3, 2001, he and fiancé Yvette were in a near-fatal explosion. Up north for the holiday, Marshall lit the propane tank in his mobile home; the hot water heater exploded, resulting in a fire. His injuries were so severe that he lay in a medically-induced coma for three months in the Blodgett Burn Unit, followed by almost eight weeks at Mary Free Bed, then went home and continued therapy. The accident also caused severe burns on Yvette's feet; she was six months pregnant, and the trauma sent her into early labor and delivery. Yvette was treated at Metropolitan Hospital while baby Jada was at Helen DeVos Children's Hospital. The accident necessitated Marshall's retirement from the school system.

"When you think you're never going to walk or talk again," says Marshall, "it makes you really appreciate life, appreciate every day."

Fast forward to 2008. Marshall is a Deacon at Messiah Missionary Baptist Church where Dawn Anderson, a fellow member of the church and also a social worker at D.A. Blodgett-St. John's, asks the membership to begin an Amachi Program. As an Amachi mentor, an adult is paired with a youth, about 10-13 years old, whose parent(s) are incarcerated. Marshall signed on as a mentor.

"The main goal of the program is to introduce the kids to Christ," says Marshall. "In addition, we give them the love, support and direction a parent would. We're not counselors in this role, although about half of our mentors have education in counseling, social work and business. We're their friend, their example."

The commitment is for at least two hours a week for about a year. Marshall's Amachi child, and he's had several, becomes a member of the family, coming over to his home for meals after church to play ball or video games and visiting Marshall's parents, grandparents and mother-in-law.

"D.A. Blodgett-St. John's is great about giving us tickets to go to the Boat Show, the Car Show, Whitecaps games, hockey games, lots of places in

Marshall (right) with his Little Brother, Phillip

the community," says Marshall. "The kids also love trips to the library and to Schuler Books & Music. At Christmas time we don red hats and make deliveries for the Santa Claus Girls.

"Our family is blessed more than the kids from these relationships," Marshall continues. "Our youngest daughter Jada is the only child at home, and it's good for her to see how other people live, what they have to deal with. The Amachi kids challenge and broaden our West Michigan perspective. They change our lives. The love factor works."

George Lanning
Former St. John's Home Resident

When a Detroit social worker told George Lanning that he was "going to Grand Rapids and not coming back," the 15-year-old had no idea where they were taking him. Over the previous months, Child Protective Services had been searching for an appropriate place for George to live. They took him to agencies that looked like hospitals, and each time he refused to get out of the car. George would say, "This isn't fair, this isn't right. I didn't do anything to deserve this, you're not going to lock me up." After exhausting the patience of the sixth social worker assigned to his case, he was driven three hours northwest to St. John's Home.

"When we drove up to St. John's, it instantly felt like home," says George. "It looked different than all the other places I'd seen. I couldn't wait to get out of the car." George was greeted at the front door by counselor and program director Cal Wallace. "He interacted with me as a human being, not a troubled teen," says George.

Up until that point George had a tumultuous life. His parents were divorced and his father was in prison at the time of his birth in 1976. For over a decade George and his older brother Michael were bounced around between their alcohol and drug abusing parents and other family members before they were placed in a foster home in Missouri. "A wonderful family took really good care of us and we loved it," says George. "Unfortunately, a year later, our paternal grandparents, prodded by our aunt, claimed us and took us to live in their home in the Detroit area."

It became evident that the boys' grandfather was the center of the family dysfunction. "He was a military man and very violent," says George. "He didn't drink, but Grandma was drunk by 6:00 P.M. everyday and began to goad Grandpa. He beat her and I would try to stop the abuse and get beat up, in turn. It was a constant cycle."

At 15, George became a Christian and it turned his life upside down. "I realized my family experiences had nothing to do with love," says George, "and this wasn't the way other people lived. It was difficult to make sense of the lies, the violence and the craziness. I became angry and rebellious." After a final showdown with his grandfather, George went to live with their aunt and her husband. When that living situation didn't work out, his aunt called Social Services and George was taken to juvenile detention. There were no charges—George had done nothing wrong—but the authorities had nowhere else to take him.

According to George, he was a "strange kid"—scared, vulnerable and an outsider wherever he went, which included 17 schools in 15 years. He didn't know how to relate to his peers. For the first three months he was at St. John's Home, George stayed in his room, coming out only for meals and

George Lanning, 1992

classes. "I had no confidence," says George, "and couldn't comprehend that life was about living, not just surviving. I attended school on campus, read, wrote poetry and tried to make sense of my life. I didn't realize there were so many things to experience. I gradually began to trust and come out of my shell."

George says he related well to the compassionate adults at St. John's who helped him process all the negative things that had happened in his life. He credits staff members such as Deborah Wilson and Dave Bockheim for treating him as a unique and valuable person. As George matured he realized he was motivated by personal relationships. He was on his way.

After successfully completing high school, George took advantage of the four-year scholarship program offered to St. John's grads and earned his Bachelor's degree in philosophy from Calvin College. Unlike most students, however, George stayed for seven years because there was so much he wanted to learn. "I used that extended time to follow numerous passions and interests, to develop as a human being and to become part of society," says George.

After college, George discovered he was an intuitive engineer and started his own company, Integrity AVL, in 2006. He designs audio-visual-lighting systems for churches, restaurants, arenas and corporate clients. George is now married and is awed by the miracle of the couples' infant son.

Today, George Lanning is a completely different person than the wounded spirit he was at age 15. "I can't imagine where I'd be if St. John's hadn't come into my life," says George. "I certainly wouldn't have gone to college. I wouldn't have the life I enjoy today. It's amazing how powerful, caring people can steer your life."

Ann Low
Foster Child

It was with relief that 16-year-old Ann Low looked out the living room window to see three police cars and a minivan in front of her house one night in November of 2007. The officers and a Child Protective Services (CPS) worker instructed Ann and her three younger brothers to fill their backpacks with what clothes they could. The siblings were taken to KidsFirst, the emergency shelter on the campus of D.A. Blodgett-St. John's (DABSJ).

"Our father had moved to an apartment about a mile away because he could no longer handle the stress of Mom's mental illness," says Ann, now 23. "She had been physically and emotionally abusive for years, and our home was an unsafe environment. Someone placed an anonymous call to CPS and workers came two or three times to check on us, and this time we were removed."

All four Low children stayed at KidsFirst for the first few nights, then her youngest two brothers were placed together in a foster home. Ann and her oldest brother waited about two months until they were placed together in the foster home of Dan and Kay VanDyke. Two or three months later, the younger boys joined them; thus all four siblings lived together at the VanDyke home. "It made a huge difference that my brothers and I could stay together," says Ann. "Dan and Kay have big hearts for children and had been foster parents for ten years.

"The VanDykes have a large home with many bedrooms," Ann continues, "and they gave my brothers and I three bedrooms on the upper floor. It was fantastic! Three of the VanDyke's four daughters lived at home at the time, and one of them slept in her sister's room on an air mattress for over a year so my brothers and I could be together." They all felt safe in the loving environment. Ann quickly became attached to her foster family who did everything they could to make sure the Lows felt a part of their family.

Throughout her time in foster care, Ann's DABSJ case worker was Amy Venard. "Amy was with me the whole way," says Ann. "My self-esteem was low and I was very shy because I had never received positive messages about myself as I grew up. Amy helped me see my good qualities. Both Amy and the VanDykes taught me the place I want to have in the world and the value of healthy relationships. I learned that family doesn't have to be biological—they can be the people you call for help, the people you celebrate your birthdays with. I am not the same person I was when I entered foster care."

For six years, Ann was on the Advocacy Board of the Michigan Youth Opportunities Initiative, a group of youth who meet regularly to discuss issues in the foster care system based on their experiences. Advocacy

Board members also speak on panels to college classes and groups at various professional trainings to give them an inside look at the foster care system.

After the Low children had been living with the VanDykes for about a year, their father gained custody of them. Consequently, the boys moved to his new home in Ohio. Because she was halfway through her senior year of high school, Ann opted to stay with the VanDykes. "I fully intended to move to Ohio after graduation," says Ann, "but when I was awarded the *Fostering Success* scholarship, a full-ride to Aquinas College that I learned about through DABSJ, it made my choice of higher education very easy. I stayed in Grand Rapids and lived on-campus during the school year and with the VanDykes for holidays and summertime."

Foster care helped Ann move into the next phase of her life, where she could experience how the world really works. "My life has balance," she says. "The VanDykes are my family." She thrived in college, made good friends and grew emotionally and socially. Academically, Ann studied Spanish and sociology. She studied abroad in Costa Rica for a semester and did a three-month internship with a missionary family in Nicaragua, helping to run a feeding program for children. Ann loved both experiences and has a passion for Latin America.

Ann, third from left, with her family

Today Ann is a Case Manager at Bethany Christian Services, working with 15 youths from Africa and Central America who are in refugee foster care. "I think my personal experiences gave me a better understanding of what a case worker is and what kids need," says Ann. "My job has opened my eyes to lots of things and made me realize how blessed I am."

Ann points to Amy Venard and the VanDykes as mentors and role models. "DABSJ has a really positive impact on families," she says. "They do a great job of gathering a network of people with hearts for kids, and it shows. What they do for the community is invaluable."

Down Syndrome Association
of West Michigan Possibility. Promise. Potential.

Mission: *To be a resource and advocacy organization, promoting public awareness and supporting lifelong opportunities for individuals with Down syndrome and their families*

2013 Step UP for Down syndrome walk, Millennium Park, Grand Rapids

233 E. Fulton Street, Suite 124
Grand Rapids, MI 49503
616.956.3488
dsawm.org

– Down Syndrome Association of West Michigan –

Roots

In 1985 a group of six parents met in one of their basements and founded the Down Syndrome Association of West Michigan (DSAWM). These parents had the same hopes and dreams for their children with Down syndrome that all parents do–they wanted resources and support for lifelong learning, educational and recreational opportunities, employment, independent living, acceptance by the community at large and a high-standard quality of life. DSAWM is a resource and advocacy organization whose purpose is to provide support to individuals with Down syndrome, as well as to their parents, caregivers and friends, so that each individual may reach their highest potential.

Melissa Werkman, DSAWM Executive Director since 2010 says, "We envision and strive for a community that is inclusive of our members with Down syndrome as their participation in all possible aspects not only benefits them, but the community as a whole. Their access to employment, educational, civic and social opportunities helps to inform policies, reduce outdated social stigmas and misconceptions, informs developing minds and encourages patience."

What began as a means to provide parental support has evolved into an organization which has also implemented direct programming, advocacy, financial assistance and a myriad of social opportunities, not only for individuals living with Down syndrome, but the people who support them.

More Alike Than Different

Down syndrome is a genetic condition that has an occurrence rate of one in every 700 live births. It affects people of all ages, races and economic levels and occurs when an individual has three, rather than two copies of the 21st chromosome. This additional genetic material alters the course of development and causes the characteristics associated with Down syndrome which include:

- Low muscle tone
- Smaller ear canals that can lead to an increase in infections and hearing problems
- A large tongue in relation to the size of the mouth, causing swallowing difficulty and speech disorders
- Mobility and motor skill delays
- Sleep apnea
- High risk of infections
- Increased risk for type II diabetes and thyroid disorders
- Increased risk for heart valve defects and childhood leukemia

All people with Down syndrome experience cognitive delays, but the effect is usually mild to moderate and is not indicative of the many strengths and talents each individual possesses.

People with Down syndrome are active participants in educational, vocational, social and recreational activities in their communities. They are included in general education classrooms, attend college, hold jobs, have friends and marry. When socialization through inclusive communities occurs, it allows individuals with disabilities to be seen as more alike than different.

Quality education programs, a stimulating home environment, good health care and positive support from family, friends and the community help people with Down syndrome lead fulfilling lives.

Programs and Services

DSAWM serves about 450 families. Approximately 55% of its members live in Kent County and the balance live in 11 other West Michigan counties: Allegan, Barry, Ionia, Kalamazoo, Mecosta, Montcalm, Muskegon, Newaygo, Oceana, Ottawa and Van Buren.

DSAWM is affiliated with more than 400 community partners including medical professionals, educational professionals, therapists and disability organizations. These partners share in the goal to promote public awareness and support lifelong opportunities for individuals with Down syndrome and their families. Programming for members is rich and varied, including:

- The *FUNctional Fine Motor Summer Program*, taught by a licensed Occupational Therapist, improves fine motor skills for children ages 5-10.
- DSAWM partners with *iCan Shine* for a one-week *iCan Bike* program in which people with Down syndrome ages 7-20 learn how to ride a bike with adapted bicycles and spotters.

2014 iCan Bike participants and instructors

- *Tiny Dancers* gives young children the opportunity to experience and perform at Arts in Motion Dance Studio.
- Inclusive adaptive water ski clinics are offered through an affiliation with Kentwood Parks and Recreation.
- Children may participate in a four-week drama class, culminating in a spring production.
- *Tween Scene* offers activities for children ages 10-14.
- *THREADS* (Together Empowering Adults with Down Syndrome) provides recreational, educational and friendship activities for youths ages 14 and older.
- *Shape Up!* emphasizes exercise and healthy nutrition for members 14 years old and older, and *Cooking Capers* is a hands-on culinary class for members 16 and older. Both programs are sponsored by Meijer.

Family Support: Social and emotional support is provided for caregivers of individuals with Down syndrome. DSAWM volunteers make home/hospital visits in the *Parents For Parents* program. A free *Guide for New and Expectant Parents* is provided to those who receive pre- or postnatal diagnosis.

The *Member Financial Assistance* program provides up to $500 annually to offset the cost of therapies, tools and programs to assist in improving communication, motor, social and cognitive development. Family Tree Therapies provides feeding and speech therapy programming.

The *Respite Assistance* program provides $250 annually to member families for respite services, and the *Adoption Assistance* program offers $1,500 to member families who adopt a child with Down syndrome. Easter Seals provides respite care, and Indian Trails Camp provides summer camp and respite opportunities for members.

Monthly playgroups and parent coffees provide opportunities for connection. *Moms' Night Out!* and the *D.A.D.S.* (Dads Appreciating Down Syndrome) support groups are safe places for parents to ask questions and share experiences. An annual picnic is held at Tunnel Park in Holland and a holiday party is held at Frederick Meijer Gardens.

The Family Hope Foundation hosts the *Special Families Fun Fest*, a low-cost, low-stress day filled with resources and fun activities for individuals with special needs and their families. DSAWM supports this event and shares resources with the Family Hope Foundation.

Education: Information, resources and support are provided to parents and educators to ensure that individuals with Down syndrome receive a quality education in preparation for further education, employment and independent living. Seminars and conferences are hosted on relevant topics.

Awareness: DSAWM works to increase public awareness, acceptance and understanding about the abilities of individuals with Down syndrome. Presentations are made to community groups, school-aged children, educators and health-care professionals. Books related to inclusion and special education topics and books specifically for elementary-aged students about Down syndrome are purchased and distributed to educational professionals in the DSAWM service area.

The *Promoting Possibilities Program* provides resources and support to medical professionals who are involved in delivering a diagnosis of Down syndrome to new and expectant parents.

Several programs and services provide support and information to educational professionals and college students pursuing degrees in general and special education.

Communication: Information about activities, programs, resources and major events is presented in the DSAWM monthly newsletter and on the website. Content includes relevant contact information, links to resources and archived copies of newsletters. The DSAWM *Lending Library* contains invaluable resources for parents and professionals on topics such as parenting, development, teaching strategies and medical concerns. The DSAWM Facebook community allows members to ask questions about raising a child with Down syndrome.

The cast of Harold and the Purple Crayon, 2014

Advocacy: Advocacy is provided for individuals with Down syndrome on medical and legal issues. Educational advocacy is offered when parents need a consultant to assist in their child's Individualized Education Program (IEP). DSAWM assists families in finding resources and researching relevant issues.

The Arc of Kent County, an advocacy organization for children and adults with special needs, often partners with DSAWM by providing conferences, programming and services.

Funding

DSAWM receives generous support from an anonymous national private foundation. Other key donors include Amway Corporation, Meijer Corporation, Tuff Cover, Gary Vos and Mike and Sue Jandernoa. A significant portion of funding comes from DSAWM members and individual donations, bequests and memorial gifts.

In October (Down Syndrome Awareness Month) the *Step UP for Down Syndrome* walk is hosted to celebrate accomplishments of individuals with Down syndrome and foster acceptance. Family and friends obtain pledges and walk a mile at Millennium Park. New in October 2014, the *3-2-1 Harvest Run* is a moonlit 10k/5k/1 mile fun run at Pigeon Creek Park on the Lakeshore. The *Inside Outing* is an indoor, upscale mini-golf event at the JW Marriott in downtown Grand Rapids in February. Money is raised through hole sponsorship and registration fees.

Leadership and Volunteers

DSAWM employs an executive director, a program director, a development manager, a resource development assistant and an administrative assistant. It is overseen by a thirteen-member board.

Annually, the DSAWM relies on the time and talents of over 120 volunteers who assist with fundraising events and social gatherings, provide clerical work in the office, run and support programs and serve as parent support liaisons for new parents.

Vision

DSAWM seeks to be an organization that empowers its members so they may realize their potential in life and as part of a community at large; to communicate with and on behalf of members by providing resources and information based on individual needs; to promote healthy life choices and lifelong learning, and to continually improve to meet the evolving needs of its members.

The Cowden Family
Members

Like many 16-year-old girls, Allie Cowden loved music and dancing; her dream was to visit Hollywood. Her parents, Gary and Deanna, said she'd have to wait until she was 21, hoping the dream would fade. But Allie held them to it, so in April 2014 the Cowdens headed to California. Gary told Allie that Radio Disney didn't offer tours, but Allie contacted the studio and made arrangements herself. The highlight of Allie's trip was sitting next to the disk jockey and announcing the upcoming song over national airwaves.

Allie was born on October 9, 1992, in Peoria, Illinois. Learning that their newborn daughter had Down syndrome was traumatic for the Cowdens, but someone from the Heart of Illinois Down Syndrome Association soon contacted them, and they received invaluable support.

When Gary had a job opportunity in West Michigan, the Cowdens were relieved to find DSAWM. They chose their new community based on educational opportunities for Allie and their son Dan, born in 1994. The Lowell Special Education Director shared the Cowdens' philosophy of inclusion, and Allie was the district's first inclusion student when she began kindergarten in 1998. The road was not always smooth; challenges were faced almost every year to secure the appropriate level of classroom support, one year with an advocate through West Michigan Inclusion Network.

"It's important to be connected with people who have the right mindset," says Deanna. "Everyone said Allie needed to be included, and I'm thankful that those seeds were planted. I've told teachers to never underestimate what Allie can learn. She always felt part of the group, and I think her classmates learned a lot from her, too." With a desire to impart that philosophy to others, Deanna volunteered with DSAWM to meet with new parents and organized events and activities.

"We can look back and see that inclusion was the right approach," says Gary. "Being with typical learners has paid huge dividends. Allie's classmates may be her employers one day. She's working and interacting with the community on a daily basis." While in high school, Allie received on-site training at various local businesses. Her performance was so impressive at McDonald's that she was asked to stay, and she's worked there for five years. "I'm a hard worker, and I get paid," says Allie. She saves some money and treats herself with clothes, Demi Lovato CDs and pizza.

While federal law mandates special education services up to age 21, Michigan extends benefits until age 26. The Lowell district contracts services through Grand Rapids Public Schools. Allie attends Kent Vocational Options where she receives daily living skills instruction and works at job sites. DSAWM was one of Allie's rotations this year, which allowed her to broaden her skills, typing articles and helping in the office. Allie is an enthusiastic learner. "I go to college, and I get homework too!" she says. Noorthoek Academy, a program for students with mild cognitive impairments, partners with Grand Rapids Community College. Allie walks in by herself and texts her parents a code word when she gets to class.

When Deanna served on the DSAWM Board, she and other parents expanded programs for older members. The THREADS (Together Empowering Adults With Down Syndrome) group provides recreational and educational activities for Allie and her friends. Conferences concentrate on issues such as self-advocacy and independence. "As long as we feel her safety isn't jeopardized," says Gary, "we give Allie as much independence as possible." Allie enjoys DSAWM dances and bowling and movie nights. She and her core group of girlfriends are eager to live independently. Their parents have discussed building a house for them and hiring a house mom. Employees from network180 come into the homes of young adults with special needs to teach life skills such as cooking and doing laundry.

The Cowdens set the bar high for Allie. She studied ballet and tap dancing at Ada Dance Academy and now trains at Arts in Motion. Her troupe performed a number choreographed by Allie at Grand Rapids Festival 2014. As an equine acrobat Allie learned to stand up on a moving horse. She swims at the YMCA and became an avid skier through Cannonsburg Challenge Ski Association. Allie lights up when she talks about

DSAWM's Shape Up!, a wellness program sponsored by Meijer for teenagers and young adults. Each session includes 45 minutes of aerobic exercise and 45 minutes of instruction. Students weigh in weekly and learn to be accountable for their choices. At home Allie records the foods she eats in a journal, assists in meal planning and reminds her family to make wise choices.

"Sometimes God puts things in your life that don't make sense at the time," says Deanna, "but He does have a path in mind. It's comforting to know there's someone who's been there before us in the DSAWM community."

The Doyle Family
Members

Two of eleven-year-old Liam Doyle's favorite things are dressing up in costumes and riding in his father Brian's horse and buggy. One Saturday morning he had the idea to combine both activities, suggesting that Brian dress up as Superman while he dressed up as Batman. Since Alto roads are usually deserted at 7:00 a.m., Brian acquiesced. However, soon the buggy was stopped by a volunteer fireman. This was the day of Alto's 5K race, and the superheroes were asked to wait until the runners passed. To add insult to injury, Brian's Superman cape had become tangled in the wheel, and all eyes were on him as he dislodged it.

"Liam's sense of wonder and spontaneity has brought so much laughter into our lives," says mom Cheryl.

Brian and Cheryl Doyle felt their family was complete with their four children: Erin, Patrick, Regan and Molly. But before their oldest child Erin left for college in 2002, they shared with their children at a restaurant that there were not six, but seven Doyles at the table. An ultrasound showed no abnormalities, and the Doyles declined amniocentesis because of the risk of spontaneous miscarriage.

"When Liam was born," says Brian, "I noticed that his eyes were slanted and his ears seemed a bit smaller than normal. The nurses wouldn't meet my eyes when I asked them if everything was okay. Our doctor told us that Liam had Down syndrome (DS). He was such a comfort because his own daughter had special needs, and he told us about the various services that existed."

"Some relatives reacted with despair when we shared the news," says Cheryl. "But when our children came to the hospital they asked, 'Why are you crying? We have kids with DS at school and Liam is going to be okay.' " In this role reversal, the Doyles' children provided comfort because of their prior experiences. In Brian and Cheryl's day, people with DS were not included in schools or community programs.

A social worker gave the Doyles a resource book from the Down Syndrome of West Michigan (DSAWM). "We devoured it," says Brian. "So much in the book was helpful. We needed to grieve for the child we thought we'd have and readjust to the child we were given."

"It's overwhelming to navigate all the resources and programs when you have a child with DS," says Cheryl, "but it's wonderful to have an organization like DSAWM that provides so much assistance."

The Doyles have benefitted from DSAWM's workshops throughout the years. Topics have included reading strategies, behavior modification and health issues. Family Tree Therapies, a Grand Rapids based multidisciplinary pediatric therapy clinic, presented at a recent conference. "We learned so much," said Cheryl, "and we are so thankful that Liam is now making steady progress with his speech and sensory issues."

Finding the right educational environment for Liam has been a challenge. Because of sensory issues, Liam becomes frustrated and shuts down in noisy classroom situations. He also has celiac disease, a chronic digestive disorder common to people with DS, and many foods at school exacerbated this condition. Cheryl currently educates Liam at home, although he attends Lowell Public Schools for music, physical education and speech services. Liam has received weekly developmental and educational therapy from the Encourage Institute for Teaching and Learning for the past two years.

"Lacey Charboneau does a tremendous job as Program Coordinator for DSAWM," says Cheryl. "She wants the best for every child." In a recent drama production that Lacey coordinated, Liam was thrilled to play a pirate. He also enjoys DSAWM's Tween Scene, available for 10-14 year olds, which provides recreational activities such as bowling and gymnastics. Even as a young boy, Liam enjoyed a weekend at Indian Trails Camp, a respite facility the Doyles learned about from DSAWM.

Liam swims and plays floor hockey through Special Olympics in the winter. In the spring he plays baseball in the Challenger Division of the Hudsonville Little League team, comprised of 8-15 year-olds with special needs. Liam enjoys showing Hocus, his constant companion, at the Kent County 4-H Fair in Lowell. Through DSAWM Liam participated in a group music therapy program at the Franciscan Life Process Center in Lowell, where he also receives individual adaptive music lessons. "Occasionally Liam sits his Barbie and Ken dolls on the piano, and he and his instructor compose songs for them," says Brian.

Brian is part of the DSAWM D.A.D.S. group. Dads meet monthly at a local restaurant, and professional speakers are brought in to discuss pertinent topics ranging from social behavior to financial planning.

"Liam's spiritual insights constantly amaze me," says Cheryl. "One day he prayed to see 'the power of God today.' That afternoon a rainbow came out and he said, 'There's the power of God I prayed for!' Liam slows down our hectic lives and helps us see that there's beauty all around us. Whenever he sees the stars, we always have to stop and sing *Twinkle Twinkle Little Star*. Even when it's -10°, it never gets old for him."

The Estrella Family
Members

Naun and Diane Estrella met while Diane was teaching at the Santiago Christian School in the Dominican Republic. They fell in love, married and had three daughters: Ana, Liliana, and Alicia. When Elias was born in December of 2003 a doctor suspected he had Down syndrome, but the hospital was not equipped to administer a definitive test. The Estrellas would have to wait for this test until their next trip to the United States. Meanwhile, Elias thrived and met most early developmental milestones on schedule.

Diane and Elias flew to Grand Rapids, her hometown, in June of 2004; tests confirmed that Elias had DS. Spectrum Hospital immediately referred Diane to DSAWM. "We were amazed at DSAWM's response and at all of their resources," says Diane. "It was such a relief to know that such an organization existed, and that I had someone to talk to who understood."

When the Estrellas returned to the Dominican Republic they faced the reality that most of these resources were not available in their home country, but the Estrellas received support and encouragement from a family whose daughter has DS. DSAWM newsletters provided information about workshops that were being offered as well as programs that would be available on successive summer visits. Naun and Diane stayed connected through the Internet and ordered resources online.

A morning in March 2010 began like any other day. Elias went to school, but by noon he was lethargic and would not eat. Blood tests indicated abnormalities including an extremely low hemoglobin count. The doctor suspected Elias had leukemia and said he would receive better care in the United States. Elias' hemoglobin counts were too low for travel, so friends lined up outside the hospital to donate blood. Two days later after two transfusions, Naun, Diane, and Elias flew to Grand Rapids, and Elias immediately began treatment at Helen DeVos Children's Hospital. Circumstances indicated that if they had waited even 24 hours, they would have lost their son. Again the DSAWM stepped up to help, lining up resources and providing vouchers for services.

Elias received chemotherapy treatments for 3½ years and spent much of the first year at the hospital. "Shortly after beginning treatment a port was put in," says Diane. "Elias knew he'd get a poke at each visit, and he fought it every time, but the Child Life staff helped him get through it by encouraging him and distracting him with toys." Treatments continued through July of 2013.

"Even though he suffered," says Naun, "he was always happy. His positive attitude made us stronger."

Diane's cousin provided a furnished home in Hudsonville, which turned out to be providential; the Grandville Christian School staff and community were welcoming and loving to the Estrellas. After Elias' fist year, Naun and Diane became aware of additional resources and services that were available for him through Hudsonville Public Schools. "When I observed the Cognitively Impaired (CI) classrooms at Hudsonville Public," says Diane, "I left in tears. I knew it was the right place for Elias. The staff is fabulous. I can't put into words how incredible the culture is. Inclusion is imprinted on everyone's hearts."

Elias' blood levels are now checked monthly. Checkups take an hour, but the Estrellas block off three hours because there is so much that Elias loves at the Helen DeVos Children's Hospital. Security guards return his salutes; volunteers play video games and putt-putt golf with him; Elias serves staff the concoctions he pretends to make in the kitchen, and the Child Life library is stocked with his favorite books.

Photo courtesy of Janel Pierson Photography

Annual highlights for the Estrella family include DSAWM's picnic and the holiday party at Frederick Meijer Gardens. In DSAWM's spring 2014 drama production, Elias played the part of a guard, sporting a breastplate and armed with a sword. "It's at these events that we make connections," says Diane. "It's reassuring to find out that our kids have a lot in common. The DSAWM staff have huge hearts and understand that families who have kids with DS have additional expenses. They're intentional about making services available to the entire community and have given me the opportunity to build relationships with Spanish-speaking residents." Diane and her daughters help with translation at events, and Diane provides rides to Spanish-speaking families.

The Estrellas have received support from many organizations in the community. At Sensory Friendly Films, funded by the Autism Society, families enjoy the studio experience without worrying about their children's extra chatting and tendency to roam. The Leukemia Society helped with expenses and invited Elias to Camp Catch-A-Rainbow. One of Elias' favorite places is Noogieland, the fantasyland play area at Gilda's Club. He is on a soccer team that is coached by the parents of two children with special needs and plays baseball on Hudsonville's Challenger team.

"Elias has taught us a lot about forgiveness, patience and compassion," says Diane. "He seems to have a radar that finds people who show amazing kindness. Through him, we have met so many people who have enriched our lives, and we have been so blessed."

The Feaster Family
Members

Even before Dennis and Sarah Feaster were ready to start a family, they shared the hope of international adoption. As social workers, they were aware that many children with challenging circumstances needed nurturing homes. They agreed that adopting a child with Down syndrome (DS) was a natural choice for them.

After their daughter Emily was born in 2001, the Feasters looked into programs at Bethany Christian Services, and in 2006 they traveled from their home in Kentucky to Hong Kong to welcome eighteen-month-old Nok-Hang, whom they named Benjamin (Benji). Besides having DS, Benji also had significant health issues that required several surgeries. "When Benji was recovering from surgeries," says Sarah, "we provided safe, loving care, and he bonded with us quickly."

The Feasters felt their family of four was complete. But in the middle of one night, as Dennis was tube-feeding Benji, he looked at his son and wondered, *If Benji were not with us, who would be caring for him?*

The plight of orphans with disabilities drove Dennis to pursue his PhD in this field. Bethany connected him with orphanages in China, and the Feasters moved to China in 2009 so Dennis could conduct research. Dennis and Sarah also considered this an opportunity to connect to Benji's culture, but Benji had difficulty in this new environment and began to regress.

About a month before the Feasters planned to return home, an orphanage asked them to foster a four-month-old baby girl with DS. "This turned out to be our saving grace," said Sarah. "It was the best thing that could have happened, to Benji especially. We all fell in love with this little girl." When it was time to return home, leaving Jia Yu was excruciating. Upon their return, they began the arduous process to adopt her.

When Dennis had a job opportunity in Michigan, Sarah contacted Down Syndrome Association of West Michigan (DSAWM) to inquire about inclusion environments in area schools. "We moved to Holland," says Dennis, "because it seemed that the community was extremely intentional in providing opportunities for people with DS."

In 2010 Jia Yu's adoption was complete, and the family traveled to China for the joyful reunion. They named their daughter Piper. During Piper's final medical exam in China, Dennis recalls, "The doctor looked at Piper, then she looked at us. She asked, 'Do you know that your daughter has Táng shì zònghé zhēng (the Chinese word for DS)?' She then asked, 'When did she get it?' This may sound shocking, but there are misconceptions in our culture as well regarding people with disabilities. In my work I knew that some people with disabilities lived in their parents' basements for decades. In regard to individuals with DS, many people remark about their loving natures, but this does not do justice to the whole person. Just like everyone, they display the full range of emotions."

Now an active 10-year-old, Benji's interests lean toward firefighters, police officers and soldiers. He imagines himself a detective, often using a paintbrush to "dust for prints." Benji attends Black River Public School, a charter school with a Montessori elementary program. "DSAWM supplied the resources to allow Benji to be integrally involved in a classroom," says Dennis. "They've ensured that this will continue across the course of his life. He has relationships with people in the community, which is a huge protective factor."

Sarah says, "The staff provides support, but knows when to encourage independence." Last year the school observed World Down Syndrome Day on March 21 (named after trisomy 21, or a third copy of chromosome 21 which causes DS). Students wore bright colored printed socks, teachers talked to students about DS and a pizza party was thrown for Benji. Emily, who also attends Black River Public School, is the biggest advocate for her younger siblings. Because she is aware of common misconceptions, she has been a gentle defender of classmates with challenges. Now four years old, Piper displays an artistic flair and loves books and puzzles. She is thriving at the Great Start Readiness Program, where she receives excellent education and therapy that is uniquely suited to her needs.

DSAWM provides financial assistance for expenses that are not covered by insurance. Benji and Piper have benefitted from their experiences at Holland's Renew Therapeutic Riding Center.

"People with DS function at a higher level than people realize," says Sarah. She has made it her mission to assist other parents in education advocacy by serving on DSAWM's Programming Committee, volunteering for DSAWM's Parent Mentoring Program and participating at Moms' Night Out. "It's invaluable to meet with others who understand the special challenges we face," she says. "We don't know what the future holds, but it's comforting to know that DSAWM has resources and workshops to assist us in the next stages of our kids' lives."

"The adoption of Benji became a gateway for another world that we did not know existed," says Dennis. "Our lives have been enriched in ways could never have imagined."

Photo courtesy of Blair Ross Jr. Photography

The Weisenborn Family
Members

When Aaron and Aimee Weisenborn's son Alex was born he was whisked away for further testing because of low Apgar scores. An hour later their OBGYN informed them that their newborn's physical markers indicated he might have Down syndrome.

Although Aimee had had positive experiences with people with Down syndrome through Special Olympics volunteer work, she recalls that it was difficult to hear that their son might have DS. "I thought it meant Alex would have a shorter life expectancy, and I wondered, *How will I raise this child to lose him?* The genetics department cleared up this misconception." Then came the news that Alex had a heart murmur, which overshadowed the DS diagnosis. Alex spent time in the Neonatal Intensive Care Unit, and his cardiologist mapped out a surgical plan. In the meantime the genetics department confirmed the DS diagnosis and connected the Weisenborns to the Down Syndrome Association of Greater St. Louis (DSAGSL).

When she returned home from the hospital, Aimee received encouragement from the mother of a child with DS, a DSAGSL member. Alex began in-home occupational therapy and had successful heart surgery at five months. The Weisenborns formed relationships with DSAGSL families and attended workshops on topics relevant to parenting a child with DS. Grateful for what they had gained, Aaron and Aimee served as Parent For Parent volunteers so that they could offer reassurance to new parents.

When a professional opportunity allowed the Weisenborns to move to Michigan in 2013, their first phone call was to the DSAWM. Through further correspondence with the DSAWM's Facebook community, they decided to settle in Hudsonville because of positive reports about the school district. After they moved they became actively involved in the DSAWM community, again volunteering in the Parent For Parent program. "I found it very helpful to be connected with a mom when Alex was born, and it's personally rewarding for me to talk with new moms," says Aimee. "Everybody has a unique story, and hearing those stories gives you a different perspective. Doctors and family members support us, too, but there's a tie that binds us as parents, and it's a safe place to ask questions."

"There are things you learn as a parent of a child with DS that you can't learn from a book," adds Aaron. "We're all on the same journey, but we don't have to blaze our own trail. Someone at DSAWM has already done that for us, so we need to pool our resources and work together." In the D.A.D.S. support group, Aaron and other fathers share information about raising children with DS and discuss how they can raise awareness. Aaron is working with others to organize the inaugural Harvest Run, a fundraiser scheduled for October 2014.

DSAWM conferences have provided guidance on topics such as

respite care, Special Needs Trust planning, and contingency planning for guardianship. Deciding who should become a child's guardian in the case of untimely death is difficult for any parent, but parents of special needs children need to construct a plan that accounts for possible guardianship beyond adulthood. The Weisenborns have connected with other DSAWM families at drama productions, the holiday party at Frederick Meijer Gardens and play dates at Java Gym in Grand Rapids and Deanna's Playhouse in Holland. Family and friends came from all over to join them in the Step UP Walk. "Our friends who don't have kids told us afterwards that they would be less afraid to have a child with DS," says Aimee.

At three years old, Alex loves Elmo and anything with a steering wheel. When he hears a catchy tune he breaks out in an enthusiastic dance, even to an audience at the downtown Farmers Market. "Alex is a typical 'threenager'," says Aaron. "Everywhere we go, people know him. I think he's touched more people in his first three years than most people touch in a lifetime." This fall a Hudsonville Public School bus will pick Alex up for preschool. The half-day program focuses on language development and school readiness. A paraprofessional and therapists will support the classroom teacher.

The Weisenborns are intentional about raising awareness about DS in the broader community. Aaron has assisted in updating training content and format for the Parent For Parent program. In the St. Louis hospital, medical personnel connected expectant parents to the DSAGSL when they were informed of prenatal testing results, largely due to the efforts of DSAGSL board members who were physicians as well as parents of a child with DS. The Weisenborns hope to see similar progress in the West Michigan medical community, as many DS pregnancies are terminated.

"It's about making a balanced decision," says Aimee. "Maybe life will be difficult for this child, but every child struggles. Parents need to hear a hopeful message. Alex has taught me the difference between aspiration and inspiration. Aaron and I have aspired to reach many goals, but when Alex came into our lives he taught us about inspiration. Before Alex was born we talked about how to prepare our child for the world, but now we realize that we also needed to prepare the world to get ready for Alex. We can't imagine our family any other way, and we're privileged that DSAWM is walking alongside us. You have no idea when you might need something, but you also have no idea what you can give unless you become involved."

PREGNANCY CRISIS AID

Mission: *HELP Pregnancy Crisis Aid, Inc. is a Catholic, nonprofit organization which is dedicated to helping pregnant women, regardless of faith, origin or background, carry their babies to term by offering support and alternatives to abortion.*

705 Bridge Street NW
Grand Rapids, MI 49504
616.450.9139
helppregnancy.org

– Help Pregnancy Crisis Aid –

Roots

The Right to Life movement was born in the years before the U.S. Supreme Court *Roe vs. Wade* decision that legalized abortion in America on January 22, 1973. After a 1971 rally in Lansing, Michigan's capital, Grand Rapids Right to Life (GRRTL) was formally organized. Judie Brown, a Grand Rapids mother of six children, joined the local group in 1972 to lend her support to the effort. At one of the first meetings, members discussed the idea of helping mothers in crisis situations carry their babies to term. Judie, who had recently met a pregnant 19-year-old who was considering an abortion, immediately jumped on the idea. With the help of a few friends, Judie founded "Alternatives to Abortion—HELP" later that year.

HELP was first located at 807 Bridge Street, then moved into available space at St. Isidore's Parish on Sweet Street NE. By January 2003, HELP moved to its current location at 705 Bridge Street NW.

For over forty years the nonprofit has provided services to thousands of individuals and families who have experienced an unplanned pregnancy. Although HELP has a tradition of Roman Catholic philosophy and viewpoint, it is nondenominational; people of other faiths volunteer and are served. HELP aspires to build relationships that respect the gift of all human life and the dignity of every person.

Goals and Programs

In keeping with its mission, HELP's goal is to promote the healthy development of babies from conception through age two—the most crucial years of life. Additionally, it strives to ensure that every client will leave HELP feeling more empowered to make informed decisions.

HELP has developed a number of programs to meet its goals. Information about health, sexuality and pregnancy is available, as well as free and confidential pregnancy testing. In a loving way the agency fosters the teachings of the Catholic Church on chastity, marriage and contraception. The Knights of Columbus recently donated a state-of-the-art ultrasound machine and, because of the expertise of a volunteer medical director, HELP is able to expand its

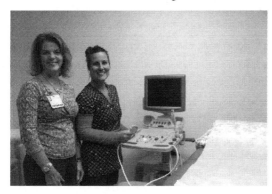

Medical Director Kim Barrows, M.D. and ultrasound technician Lori Potter

capabilities in this area. Statistics show that women who see their prenatal babies on a sonogram—in the setting of a medical clinic where they are building a positive relationship—are unlikely to have an abortion. Women have the opportunity to select maternity clothing and, just prior to giving birth, each mother is provided a layette of baby essentials, which enables her to be prepared to take the baby home from the hospital.

HELP, the walk-in program, provides formula, food, diapers, clothing and other essentials on a monthly basis until the child's second birthday. Clients are linked to community resources related to pre- and postnatal care, adoption, housing, food pantries and legal or social services. HELP also supports women who struggle with the aftermath of abortion by connecting them with support services within the community, such as Project Rachel and Surviving the Secret. These services provide encouragement and healing from abortion-related trauma.

Moms with layettes of baby essentials

Through the *Loving Arms Program*, expectant and recent mothers set up scheduled appointments to view instructional DVDs on a wide range of topics such as health, sexual integrity, childcare, development and discipline. This incentive-based program awards points to the client that are exchanged for baby and personal care items that can be chosen from the *Loving Arms Boutique*.

The *Safe Sleep* Program was developed in the fall of 2013 to provide a Pack 'n Play to any parent without a crib for their infant, ensuring peace of mind that baby is safe while sleeping.

The Wright Connection

Opened in June 2011 and located in what was once a vacant, run-down space adjacent to HELP's offices in the same building, the Wright Connection is a community gathering place named in honor of Susan Wright, a wife and mother with deep pro-life values who lost her battle with breast cancer in 1999. In the Wright Connection, HELP hosts educational programs on issues impacting families in a relaxed, contemporary atmosphere. Young mothers develop friendships and connect with resources and experts through classes and programs on relevant topics such as prenatal care, nutrition, lactation, childbirth, parenting, child development, faith formation, post-abortive support and postpartum depression. Non-judgmental and confidential peer counseling addresses the physical, emotional and spiritual issues that accompany parenting.

Cradles of Grace Ministry provides one-on-one mentoring to single pregnant women. This ministry encourages life transformation through the love of Christ and helps build a community of support. The *Safe from the Start* Program works with Spectrum Health's Healthier Communities to promote healthy eating and exercise programs and complements HELP's Childbirth/Breastfeeding classes. Offered by the Kent County Health Department at the Wright Connection, the *Safe Sleep* presentation gives families the latest information on keeping babies safe in the home.

The future is bright at the Wright Connection as more educational options become available. They include *After Abortion*, a bimonthly post-abortion support group; Davenport University's Vita program, which provides low-income tax assistance; the addition of a fatherhood component to the *Safe from the Start* program and women's Bible Studies. The Wright Connection also has many opportunities for community involvement.

Expectant and new mothers attend classes in The Wright Connection.

The Garden of Life

In 2011 long-time volunteer Sandy Lowery and her husband John purchased the empty lot next door to HELP on Bridge Street and spent over a year transforming the space into a beautiful "Garden of Life." The Garden is an oasis of green in a neighborhood of storefronts, an unexpected delight for neighbors and passersby alike. HELP takes pride in its appearance and the

Garden gives the property a homey, completed feel. Plans have recently been announced for further redevelopment in the near-West side neighborhood, and, combined with the Garden of Life, HELP is a forerunner to that urban renewal.

Staff and Volunteers

Currently over 400 clients are served every month at HELP, and its doors are opened Monday through Thursday because of the active involvement of about fifty volunteers. Client advocates mentor young women who face difficult circumstances and are in need of guidance. Bilingual advocates counsel Spanish-speaking clients on a one-on-one basis or assist a trained client advocate with translations. Office assistants/receptionists complete general office tasks such as copying, filing, sorting forms and setting up new appointments for clients. Clothing sorters are behind-the-scenes volunteers who wash and sort the material goods donated to HELP, while others enjoy stocking the *Loving Arms Boutique* or creating layettes to be offered to the mothers of newborns.

Items always in demand are formula, diapers, onesies, socks, blankets, maternity clothing, infant and children's winter clothing, and baby equipment such as Pack-'n-Plays, bassinets, strollers, gates, swings, and exersaucers. HELP relies on the goodness of the community to provide these items.

HELP's annual GenerosiTee Golf Outing is successful due to the efforts of many volunteers as well as the participation of the golfers.

Leading the volunteers are a director and program coordinator. An eight-person board of directors meets quarterly to review the director's report, go over financial data and oversee major purchases and programming changes. Over the years HELP has had medical directors on a part-time, volunteer basis. Currently, Medical Director Kimberly Barrows M.D. is very involved with the agency.

Partners and Affiliations

HELP collaborates with community partners Spectrum Health Healthier Communities, Cradles of Grace, Kent Country Great Start Parent Coalition, Knights of Columbus, Catholic Charities West Michigan and Aquinas College's Project Unite. It is also in good standing with Heartbeat International and the National Institute of Family and Life Advocates.

Funding

HELP is funded by private donations, various Knights of Columbus Councils and local parishes. Three annual fundraisers also raise operating capital: *Noto's Charity Wine Fest*, an elegant winter evening of wine tasting, gourmet Italian cuisine, wine/culinary auction and live entertainment; the *GenerosiTee Golf Outing* held in July; and the *Fall Dinner* which features a social hour, dinner and an inspirational speaker. Growth at HELP is on a steady, upward trajectory.

Vision

Why should a pregnant woman, unsure of her desire to give birth, come to HELP? The answer is that the staff and volunteers at HELP *Listen, Acknowledge, Accept, and Provide,* or *L.A.A.P.* for short. "We've done a great job over the years to provide material assistance to mothers," says Director Paula Veneklase. "But we also want to make sure women know that we support them holistically, that we are building relationships, that we are here for them. Our desire is that the services at HELP are caring and accepting for women who experience unexpected pregnancies. We strive to *plant seeds of hope* and allow God's love to influence the hearts and minds of all who enter our doors."

Judie Brown
Founder

Before the 1973 Roe vs. Wade decision was handed down by the United States Supreme Court, the abortion issue was hotly debated throughout the country. During that time, Judie Brown and her teenage son Chris hosted a booth at a Ludington summer fair with literature about a referendum on Michigan's 1972 fall ballot which, if passed, would allow abortion through the fifth month of pregnancy. At the booth Judie used large-scale photographs of babies developing in their mothers' wombs to explain the various stages of fetal development. One young woman lingered, looking very sad. When Judie asked if she was all right, the young woman indicated she would like to speak privately.

Chris took over the booth, and Judie and "Mindy," as Judie imagined her name to be, talked. Mindy related that her only sister, the "shining star" of the family, had become pregnant out of wedlock and it had destroyed their family. In fact, during one heated family argument, her father pushed her sister, who fell down the stairs. Shortly thereafter, her sister miscarried. Their father kicked her out of the house, and Mindy had not seen her sister since. Now, a few years later, Mindy was also pregnant and unmarried. She planned a trip to Detroit the next day for an abortion.

"The photos I was showing made her want to change her mind," says Judie, "but she didn't know what to do. Could I help her? I didn't know what to say. I finally suggested she call Catholic Social Services in Muskegon. She said she wasn't Catholic. I told her to contact them anyway and gave her money for the phone call."

Judie never learned if Mindy delivered the baby or not, but she realized that day that it wasn't enough to say that abortion is wrong. "We need to say, 'we care about you and your problems' and do something concrete to help," says Judie.

So when the subject of supporting pregnant women was brought up at a local Right to Life meeting a few weeks later, Judie was eager to "take the ball and run with it," as she says. *Alternatives to Abortion— HELP* was born. "We purposely had our name begin with the letter A," says Judie, "so we would be the first telephone number people found in the

Judie Brown, 1975

Yellow Pages when they turned to 'Abortion.' "

HELP's first location was at 807 Bridge Street. Friend Casey Sak rented the building to Judie for $40 per month, and Judie's husband Adrian and their children painted the office. Friends Rita Gillis, Rosemary Alt and Jan Czkowski took charge of procuring baby supplies. John Alt showed up one day with a hearse filled with diapers. Helen Olsen volunteered as secretary. Bishop Joseph Breitenbeck donated an answering machine. Two obstetricians/gynecologists, Drs. Miles Murphy and Larry Burns, gave free professional medical care to any woman HELP referred to them. "One time I stopped by their office and realized that nine of the eleven women in their waiting room were from HELP," says Judie.

She continues, "We printed brochures to let people know we were open and ready to help needy moms with diapers and clothing for their babies. A friend who was a nurse at St. Mary's Hospital distributed our brochures. We put flyers and pamphlets everywhere. I contacted other agencies to let them know we were available. We grew through word of mouth."

Although HELP follows the philosophy and perspective of the Roman Catholic Church, Judie intentionally made the agency nondenominational because of Mindy. "We have always been independent of the Church," says Judie.

At the time Judie was building and developing HELP, she and Adrian had six children. From the beginning, Adrian was "my right arm, my backup," she says. During her 11 years leading HELP, Judie gave birth to two more children. In addition, she and Adrian adopted three children, two of whom were pregnant teens. They fostered 27 children, many unwed mothers, through Catholic Social Services. Many young women stayed with the Browns to complete their pregnancies, then gave up their babies for adoption. "Everyone collects something; we collect people," Judie jokes. "It was a life that made us very happy. My kids grew up knowing we had to do more than take care of ourselves—we had to reach out and help others. They knew everyone was welcome at our home."

She praises those who have taken over HELP the past 30 years. "God has used the many employees and volunteers as His hands, His feet, His heart and His voice. They have done a wonderful job of expanding services and adding the educational component. I am very proud of HELP and what it does for mothers without resources to save precious lives."

Donna Miller
Volunteer

Anthony Queen
Client

The words of Mother Teresa of Calcutta resonate in Donna Miller's heart: "In this life we cannot do great things. We can only do small things with great love."

When her younger child left for college, Donna felt the call to volunteer by helping young mothers and their babies. After she investigated a few possibilities that weren't a good fit for her, Donna opened the Yellow Pages of the telephone book. The first agency she noticed was "Alternatives to Abortion—HELP Pregnancy Crisis Aid." She went in to find out how she could be involved and began training for the position of client advocate that same day. That was 24 years ago.

As a client advocate Donna meets with mothers who come to HELP for baby supplies. She's seen young women cry with relief to receive a 12-pack of diapers. An even bigger part of Donna's job is to listen to the mothers. "They need love," says Donna. "They need someone who cares and will be there for them, no matter what is going on in their lives. So many of the women live in unhealthy situations with little or no support. Their family ties have been broken and no one seems to care for them anymore. Sometimes we pray together."

Donna forms bonds with the mothers she sees on a regular basis, some closer than others. She might go to a client's home to help, if need be. One of the women Donna met was Nicole, the mother of a new baby boy named Kaden. When Donna heard of Nicole's death a few weeks later, she contacted the infant's father, Anthony Queen, who planned to raise his son alone.

"Donna encouraged me to meet her at HELP," says Anthony. "I was a first-time father at age 48, a fish out of water. I knew nothing about babies. I needed all the help I could get. Donna's call was a blessing."

The two became close. In addition to diapers, wipes, formula, and baby clothes, Donna arranged for Kaden's first formal photographs. She's also been there for the father and son on birthdays and Christmases. Most importantly, Donna is someone to whom Anthony can express the concerns and frustrations of being a parent. He relies on her knowledge on child-rearing issues. "It's so helpful to have someone with resources and experience to bounce things off," says Anthony.

Thankfully, Anthony has a more extensive support system than many of the other HELP clients. "My cousin is a nurse," he says, "and I had her on speed dial those first few months. She let me know it was okay to call her any time, day or night." Employees of Helen DeVos Children's Hospital found Kaden a pediatrician, and the members of Anthony's church,

Tabernacle Community Church, have been there for him. There are three families in particular who take turns watching Kaden on weekends so Anthony can work a second part-time job. (His full-time job is with a mortgage company. Anthony put his pursuit of a Masters' degree in Business Administration on hold when Kaden began walking; he hopes to soon reignite that goal with online studies.)

Anthony is a huge advocate of HELP. "I see lots of people who are served at HELP," he says. "I believe they would be lost individuals without it; they would have nowhere else to go. I appreciate the personal attention I receive and see other people leaving the office with happy, smiling faces. It's a good feeling when people know you and meet your needs. That would be missing without HELP."

In addition to being a client advocate, Donna has also been a member of the HELP board for 15 years and transports personal care items that the nonprofit purchases at a reduced rate. She has found meaning and joy through her countless volunteer hours. Donna says, "I feel Christ's love, a sense of being close to God, while doing this work. It has opened my eyes to all of God's kingdom and broadened my love for His people. I keep this thought from Mother Teresa in mind: 'If you judge people you have no time to love them.' "

"Kaden and HELP have been blessings in my life," says Anthony. "He's my little buddy and HELP has been another source of God's direction and guidance in my journey."

Although Kaden just turned two, Anthony continues to visit Donna and the others at HELP. He laughs, "Those ladies would have my neck if I didn't bring Kaden in for visits."

Sandy Lowery
Volunteer

In 2002 Sandy Lowery read a notice in her church bulletin asking for volunteers at HELP Pregnancy Crisis Aid. She had never heard of the agency, but as a pro-life advocate she wanted to learn more. Sandy made an appointment to explore how she might get involved and that phone call began her relationship with HELP, one that's lasted for over 12 years.

"It's one thing to be pro-life," says Sandy, "but I knew I wanted to do something concrete to support mothers who had decided to give birth to their babies." She took on the role of client advocate, whereby she meets privately with mothers (and sometimes fathers) to find out how they and their babies are doing. Sandy encourages the parents to discuss and ask questions about the educational videos they watch at HELP and, as a nurse, her medical knowledge and certification are often invaluable.

Through her experiences at HELP, Sandy's view of abortion has broadened; she has learned it's a very complicated, many-faceted issue. "It's not that the mothers don't think the life growing inside them is a baby," says Sandy. "Most do. They become abortion-vulnerable when overwhelming socio-economic problems collide with a new pregnancy. They can't see how they're going to feed their other children, pay their rent and be responsible for yet another life. Some people have very challenging situations in their lives, and that's when they might see abortion as a means of survival. By providing a support system, we try to help them understand that this child is a valuable person created by God, regardless of the circumstances of its conception."

For many years, the lot next to HELP was occupied by a rundown apartment building. When it burned down, Sandy dreamed of a lovely green space to take its place, instead of a new business that might be counter to HELP's mission, or a weedy, ill-kempt lot. Sandy's husband John bought the property for her as an anniversary gift and Sandy spent the next year turning it into a "Garden of Life."

In addition to planting grass, flowers, bushes, trees, and adding a lovely, low-profile fence, the Lowerys commissioned local artist Mic Carlson to cast a seven-foot bronze statue of *The Madonna of the Streets*. There is also a walkway that features uplifting, life-filled messages, rosary beads created with paving stones, a fountain and a statue of *Jesus with the Little Children*. The garden, dedicated in late 2012, is a place of serenity enjoyed by HELP's clients and area residents—a beautiful, quiet oasis for prayer and contemplation.

The Garden of Life is a unique green space in an area of storefronts. "People tell me how unusual it is," Sandy says, "although I didn't think of it that way as we built the garden. I'm glad people are noticing the Garden and our building. HELP takes pride in its grounds; we want it to feel home-like for the mothers." Future plans include turning an area adjacent to the Garden into a patio where the moms can mingle and support one another.

One ripple effect of Sandy's involvement with HELP has been a cadre of family and friends who donated engraved bricks and trees and also cut the grass and keep the Garden tidy each week. It's one piece in HELP's steady increase in community awareness that's resulted in more volunteers and increased donations, which, in turn, has resulted in more mothers and babies served. Through her leadership of her parish Respect Life Committee, Sandy holds periodic diaper and formula drives to benefit HELP. In this way, many more people have learned about HELP and its mission.

In 2013 Sandy was asked to become a member of the Board of Directors, a position in which she thinks she can make a further difference. "The women we serve are very appreciative of what we give them. We're a safety net when they have nowhere else to turn," says Sandy, "and I'm proud to serve on the board."

"When a person is afraid for the future," she continues, "HELP offers some hope that their situation is temporary, that things can improve. They can get past their current crisis and carry their baby to term. I love when we help clients learn to think differently and reprioritize their lives. It's not always easy to see that God has a plan for each child and that each child is a gift from God. We need to support mothers and fathers who make life-affirming decisions."

Blanca Covarrubias
Client, Volunteer, Program Coordinator

The year 2006 was memorable for Blanca Covarrubias. She became pregnant, her husband lost his job, she underwent brain surgery and she gave birth to her second child.

Born and raised in Tampico, Tamaulipas in Mexico, Blanca completed her degree in dentistry and started a practice in a poor part of town. Her father thought she was crazy, but Blanca liked helping people who really needed her. She dreamed of a better life, however, and in 1995 Blanca immigrated to the United States. She chose Grand Rapids because she had a friend who lived here.

Blanca found employment at a plastics-injection factory where she met her future husband, José. "I thought I would get my certification to practice as a dentist in Grand Rapids," says Blanca, "but found out it was too difficult and too expensive. Plus, life got in the way—I met my husband, we married and started a family."

The couple had a son in 2000, and then Blanca became pregnant with their second child in 2006. Ten weeks into the pregnancy, she was diagnosed with a brain tumor. "The doctor said he had to operate the next week, and asked if I wanted to abort the baby," says Blanca. "He said he couldn't guarantee the child would be perfect. I told him I wanted to keep my baby."

Blanca's tumor was removed and no further treatments were necessary. She had headaches for about three years afterwards, but has been medication-free since then. "I realized I had a fresh start in life," says Blanca, "and began to attend church."

When Blanca's husband lost his job a few months later, someone told her about HELP, and she went in to see what services were available. While there, Blanca overheard a woman asking questions of the staff in Spanish, but no one at HELP understood the language. So Blanca stepped in to translate. She loved the role and continued as a volunteer until she delivered her baby, another little boy. Since her husband was out of work and at home to care for the baby, Blanca went back to HELP to translate for others.

Jose found another job and Blanca had to stop volunteering at HELP temporarily, but when her younger son entered preschool she returned to HELP two half-days a week, then more frequently when he entered first grade. On her shifts Blanca worked in the *Loving Arms Boutique* and was available when Spanish-speaking clients needed a translator. She went back every day because she enjoyed it. "I was drawn to HELP," says Blanca. "When I started working with clients, I realized that helping people made me feel good."

Blanca has an effective touch with HELP's clients. One day a woman came into HELP, afraid that her friend was considering an abortion. Blanca visited the woman at her home and listened to her story. Then Blanca showed the pregnant woman a life-sized model of a three-month-old fetus. "I set it in her hand," says Blanca, "and she began to cry. She quickly changed her mind and decided to give birth to her baby." The woman gave the baby up for adoption—an open adoption—which allows her to see her child from time to time.

Blanca became so valuable to HELP that she was offered a part-time job. Then, in 2013, Blanca accepted the position of Program Coordinator. As such, Blanca works with Spectrum Health to organize and coordinate the prenatal, childbirth and breast-feeding classes offered at HELP.

"Blanca is an almost-perfect angel here on earth," says Julie Saganski, a weekly volunteer. "She is gentle, kind, loving and quiet. She never criticizes and is always helpful. I've seen Blanca interact with her sons

and she is a wonderful mother as well."

Blanca's friend Maribel became curious about HELP and began volunteering for the program in 2010. Blanca describes her friend as wary of helping people, but having a willing heart. Little by little, Maribel improved her people skills. She learned a lot and became less judgmental, according to Blanca. "HELP has changed my friend Maribel's life, too," says Blanca. "Not only is she better with people, but she is doing computer work for HELP." Blanca's sons, now 14 and 8, also volunteer at HELP on occasion.

"I've always loved helping people," says Blanca. "If I can do something for someone else, I do it. I try to encourage people to find the purpose in their lives. Every day I thank God for the opportunity to save lives at HELP. I pray, 'God, help me to help these people.' I'm in His hands."

Destiny Smith
Client

When Destiny Smith walked into HELP in April 2013, her intention was to have an abortion. Already the mother of four children and recently enrolled at Everest Institute in the Administrative Medical Assistant program, Destiny was feeling overwhelmed and unable to cope with what she considered a potential roadblock to her education. She sat down and spoke with HELP Director Paula Veneklase.

"Paula told me 'God doesn't make mistakes,' " says Destiny. "She said this was just a trial and everything would work out. Then she telephoned a technician who came in and did an ultrasound. I was eight weeks along and could see my baby moving on the screen. It was very emotional and both Paula and I were crying. I knew she really cared about *me*; it wasn't just a job to her."

Because Destiny had first gone to HELP a few years earlier on the recommendation of a friend for diapers, wipes, formula and baby clothes, she knew it was a place she could turn to in her time of need.

"I could see how desperate she was," says Paula, "but I knew in my heart an abortion would only lead to despair and not have the positive outcome she was looking for."

The ultrasound gave Destiny more time to think about her decision. "I thought if I didn't go to the doctor, the baby wouldn't seem real to me," says Destiny. So she continued with her classes at Everest and held off visiting her nurse/midwife at Cherry Street Health Services until she was five months along.

Destiny always believed and trusted in God, but "tribulations come into your life nonetheless," she says. "Paula's words of faith lifted me up, put my focus toward God."

Paula was overwhelmed with relief when she received a call from Destiny six months later, saying she would need some support when her baby was born in the coming month. "God had answered our prayers," says Paula. "When Destiny left HELP after the ultrasound that day, I didn't think she was totally convinced she could go through with the birth. I was second-guessing what I had said to her, yet realized I had done all I could to help her make an informed decision. I gave it up to prayer."

Destiny believes God was looking out for her as she finished her nine-month educational program one November afternoon. Just six-and-a-half hours later, Destiny's water broke, sending her into labor with the speedy delivery of a beautiful, healthy girl in the hospital triage area. Destiny named her infant daughter Journey to honor the journey she took during her pregnancy.

Fully committed to her educational goal, Destiny worked a three-month externship program in Dr. John Campbell's general practice medical office. She successfully finished that experience on May 7, 2014, and graduated on June 6. Her resumes were polished and sent to prospective employers, and she's hoping to find a position in her new field very soon.

Destiny continues to check in at HELP every so often to keep in touch. She feels close to Paula, and their relationship continues to grow. "She calls me by name and asks me how the other things in my life are going," says Destiny. "Not long ago I lived in a shelter for a month or so. Paula was very concerned and gave me a list of landlords to call. I let her know when I found a place to live. Right now all I have is a king-sized comforter. I am in the process of buying curtains and Paula is working with friends and colleagues to help furnish my apartment. I am so happy to have a home that I don't care if there isn't any furniture."

Paula is proud of Destiny and the choice she made to give birth to her baby. "Journey is such a sweet child and Destiny is a wonderful mother. She works hard to make a home for her children," says Paula.

Destiny says, "HELP has been a big part of my life for the past few years. I'm grateful there's such an organization because lots of mothers need help. You can rely on them when you don't have the income, and I have told other people about HELP. I am so thankful I could finish my degree and have my baby, too."

Destiny and Journey, pictured with HELP Executive Director Paula Veneklase.

Baxter Community Center

Mission: *A Christian response to human needs*

935 Baxter Street SE
Grand Rapids, MI 49506
616.456.8593
baxtercommunitycenter.org

– Baxter Community Center –

Roots

The late 1960s were a time of profound civil strife and pervasive racial inequality in America, and West Michigan was no exception. Governmental housing covenants kept black and white populations separate. The public school system segregated students. Stereotypes and suspicions inhibited communication between races.

Several members of Eastern Avenue Christian Reformed Church were moved to address the unmet needs in their neighborhood. James White, then a recent Calvin College graduate, described the neighborhood as a "wasteland, desperate for hope." Dennis Hoekstra, a Calvin College education professor, wanted to bring people and institutions together in response. White and Hoekstra combined forces to open Eastern Avenue Community Center in a location above Bierling Bakery on Eastern Avenue.

A Response to Material Needs

Baxter Christian School, located at 935 Baxter Street SE, merged with Oakdale Christian School in 1963 and closed its doors at the end of 1969. Eastern Avenue Community Center leaders arranged to occupy the building, and Baxter Community Center was officially established in its current location in the heart of the Baxter neighborhood. Young people attended the summer program in droves to play basketball and share a meal in a safe and welcoming environment. Baxter leaders continued to shape programming by responding community needs.

In the 1970s the Center became home to the Freedom School during a three-week boycott of the public school system. Riots and nightly curfews threatened to maintain division, but these turbulent times only served to solidify Baxter's identity as an organization committed to racial reconciliation. This decade saw the inception of the income tax preparation program, the food pantry and the clothing pantry.

Growth in Education, Health and Social Services

In the 1980s a child development center and medical clinic were opened; both programs experienced rapid growth. Dr. Bob Bulten and the doctors from his practice, Alger Pediatrics, volunteered their time to become the first doctors in Baxter's pediatric clinic.

At the end of the 1980s Baxter conducted its first capital campaign. Casey Wondergem of Amway Corporation organized a group of friends, including Richard DeVos, John Bouma and Ambassador Peter Secchia as the Baxter Business Advisory Committee. At their first meeting they raised a million dollars.

In 1999 the Baxter clinic became a Women, Infants and Children

(WIC) site. In 2007 the dental clinic partnered with Kent County's Strong Beginnings program to begin Brush Up For Baby, a project that provides dental care and education to at-risk pregnant women.

Melanie Beelen, Executive Director since 1995, is committed to Baxter's mission. "By our very nature," she says, "we are a compilation of a hundred different personalities and characters of such rich storylines. Our earthly presence keeps us in touch with real life challenges and successes. We need to foster humility through expecting great things and realizing we are part of a bigger piece of the puzzle in life."

Programs and Services

Baxter has four pillars on which services are based: the *Child Development Center*, the *Wholistic Health Clinic*, the *Mizizi Maji Mentoring Program* and *Marketplace*.

Mayor George Heartwell reads to CDC students

Baxter's *Child Development Center (CDC)* is a dynamic place of growth and learning for children from infancy to age 12, allowing parents to work or attend school with the knowledge that their children are safe. The CDC is licensed by the State of Michigan and has held national NAEYC accreditation. Students in the *Adventurers* Preschool room become independent thinkers who question, explore, and make discoveries about the world around them. The *Explorers* Preschool room, through a partnership with the Early Learning Neighborhood Collaborative, is aimed at expanding and sustaining high quality early care and education in vulnerable Grand Rapids neighborhoods. Children ages 15 months–3 years in the *Sparrows* room enjoy sensory experiences and field trips. *Little Lambs* (infants) enjoy new experiences each day through free play, music, reading and group learning. Before- and after-school care are available.

The *Wholistic Health Clinic* addresses the entire person, caring for the body, mind and spirit. Several of the area's finest medical practitioners regularly volunteer their services, offering affordable primary care. The clinic serves families who lack insurance or receive Medicaid or Medicare. Adult services include blood pressure screenings, nutrition coaching, diabetes testing and treatment, ADD/ADHD assessment and treatment, vision and prayer clinics and various support groups. The *Pediatric Clinic* provides well-child physicals and immunizations. Baxter has a growing partnership with the Helen DeVos Children's Hospital, which recently opened a Healthy Weight Clinic. The *Wholistic Health Clinic* partners with the Women, Infants and Children (WIC) Program to serve pregnant and postpartum women and children from birth to five years of age. Baxter's *Dental Clinic* offers high-quality dental care for those who might be unable to afford it. Services include examinations, cleanings, fillings, extractions and X-rays.

Free therapy is available for numerous issues, including depression, grief/loss, family issues, domestic abuse, traumatic life events (including rape) and ADD/ADHD. Clients facing substance abuse issues are referred to rehabilitative services such as Thresholds. Families with special needs children are referred to Ken-O-Sha, and a relationship is maintained with the Kent County Juvenile Court to address youth behavioral issues.

The *Mizizi Maji Mentoring Program* provides students ages 8-18 with group and one-to-one mentoring, supplementing family support systems. Weekly gatherings create opportunities for teamwork, volunteerism, social, cultural and historical competency building, academic excellence and college preparedness. In the *3.0 Gets To Go* program, students earn trips by maintaining solid grades along with community and extracurricular involvement. Students have traveled to Canada, Chicago, New York City, Washington D.C, Virginia Beach and South Africa to visit historical sites, universities, museums and a multitude of ethnic restaurants.

Mizizi Maji South Africa trip

The Creative Youth Center provides individual tutoring for *Mizizi Maji* and other neighborhood students. GRCC Culinary Arts students teach the art of fine dining; the college also hosts students for an annual Science Learning Night. Through the Grand Valley State University African American Studies Department, students learn in a college seminar setting and are guided on university tours. History is brought to life in the annual *Live History Museum*, hosted by Baxter students.

The *Threads* group, an adult sewing class, learns life skills and makes beautiful quilts that will stand the test of time. Field trips to museums, retreats and quilt shows further build community.

Baxter's *Marketplace* serves as a bridge for people who are preparing to move from emergency needs to self-sufficiency. Neighbors receive emergency food assistance once a month from Baxter's ACCESS food pantry and may visit the clothing pantry twice a month. Food and clothing are provided by organizations, educational institutions and individuals. Families also receive food baskets for Thanksgiving and Christmas.

Baxter's *Greenhouse* focuses on environmental awareness, food security and nutrition, and community spirit. *In the Garden* includes monthly workshops to offer practical, seasonal tips for maintaining gardens. Families in the *Neighborhood Garden* program receive, at no cost, a 4' x 8' raised garden, soil, flower and vegetable seedlings, a garden mentor and special access to classes and events. The *Greenhouse* hosts community events such as the *Strawberry Jamboree* and *Tomato Festival* and provides fresh produce to the pantry, allowing residents access to more nutritious food.

Marketplace offers *Freedom in Your Finances* classes that explore what it means to recognize God as provider and to be responsible stewards of His gifts. Through financial literacy, money management, goal setting, budgeting training and one-on-one meetings with a budget coach, participants move towards financial independence and self-sufficiency. In collaboration with the Kent County Tax Credit Coalition and AARP, Baxter's Marketplace offers *free tax preparation* to low-income families and individuals. The *Senior Moments* program is a chance for seniors to share good conversations and fun experiences. Seniors gain computer literacy and benefit from fitness classes that are sponsored by Senior Neighbors.

Funding

A majority of Baxter's support comes directly from generous contributions from individuals, places of worship and businesses. Governmental funding and client contributions defray a portion of program costs. United Way allocations and designations comprise 21% of the operating budget.

The *Opening Doors Celebration* is an annual fundraiser; individual supporters, business sponsors and community members celebrate the beauty of building community across racial, economic, geographic and generational lines. *Growing Roots* is a table-hosted event at which friends of Baxter Community Center invite others to learn about the organization.

Leadership and Volunteers

Baxter Community Center employs 42 individuals, including an executive director, program coordinators and other program staff. A twelve-member board serves the organization.

Volunteers from the neighborhood and the broader West Michigan community serve at Baxter. Colleges and universities provide student interns; mentors serve in the *Mizizi Maji Mentoring* program and the *Threads* sewing classes; doctors and dentists serve in clinics; *Marketplace* shelves are organized and stocked; planting and weeding take place in the greenhouse and garden, and neighborhood members receive free tax preparation services. On *Fix Up Day* over 100 volunteers spruce up the building and grounds to get Baxter ready for another year of service.

Partners and Affiliations

Given Baxter's history, location and impact, it is considered a great collaborative partner in various efforts in the Grand Rapids area. Through a grant from the W.K. Kellogg Foundation, the YMCA and Baxter partner to provide free physical fitness and nutrition classes. Baxter is one of the YMCA's four "Healthy Living Hubs," which serve as central locations where neighbors access fresh food and enjoy family-centered physical activity. Baxter, along with five other nonprofits (Grand Rapids African American Health Institute, the Hispanic Center of Western Michigan, GRCC, Family Outreach Center Inc., Grand Rapids Urban League and United Methodist Community House) form the Urban Core Collective, which initiated the Transformative Leadership Program to equip professional leaders in communities of color. Baxter's Early Learning Neighborhood Collaborative addresses the need for preschool readiness. The W.K. Kellogg Foundation has invested in each of these efforts.

Vision

Baxter Community Center seeks to reveal God's love by responding to human needs in its community through effective programs and partnerships. Baxter addresses neighbors' immediate needs, thereby empowering individuals to become responsible, productive and self-sufficient while affirming the positive qualities in each person and in the community.

Kessia Graves
Mizizi Maji Mentoring Program

As a sixth grader at Ridge Park Charter Academy, Kessia Graves had a life-changing conversation with her friend Raqhelle Millbrooks. Raqhelle told Kessia about a recent trip she'd taken to Ontario, Canada, through Baxter Community Center's Mizizi Maji Mentoring Program, and she invited Kessia to join the group.

The Mizizi Maji Mentoring Program has provided hundreds of young people ages 8-18 with opportunities for group and one-to-one mentoring from role models within the community. At weekly meetings a network of mentees, parents, volunteer mentors and interns engage in activities that build volunteerism, social, cultural and historical competency and college preparedness.

One of the advantages of being a member, according to Kessia, is to be a part of a group of peers that come from varied backgrounds and attend different schools. "This is a healthy environment in which we can all grow," she says. "We're all friends, and it's very non-threatening. We learn things we don't learn at school, like how to apply for scholarships and what different colleges have to offer. We know that if we get a bad grade we can work though it. Miss Sharon Lachappelle (Program Director) and our mentors offer extra encouragement.

"Because of my involvement through the years," Kessia continues, "I'm aware of opportunities that are out there. Before I was in the Mizizi Maji program I knew education was important, but now it's ingrained in me. The value of education has driven me throughout my high school experience." Mizizi Maji mentees learn that doing your best in school opens doors and offers intrinsic satisfaction, but they also earn rewards for academic success. 3.0 Gets To Go: Education Through Travel is a program component in which members who maintain at least a 3.0 grade point average during the school year and exemplify good citizenship may travel to various locales throughout the United States and Canada. Educational travel experiences build preparedness for life and social competency.

3.0 Gets To Go is funded largely through grants from Grand Rapids Youth Foundation and the Wege Foundation. On each trip, students visit museums, cultural centers and an area college. "I've learned interesting things about my culture," says Kessia, "and I've also learned important life lessons, such as how to navigate public transportation systems and implement manners by trying new foods from other cultures. When you step outside your comfort zone you see the diversity in other parts of the world."

Recently an intergenerational group—comprised of Mizizi Maji parents and students, Baxter's Senior Citizens Computer Class and the Threads sewing group—chartered a bus and traveled to the National Underground Railroad Freedom Center in Cincinnati, Ohio. On this trip, elders and youth journeyed through history and engaged in reciprocal learning. Elders shared their wisdom through old school personal interaction and youth shared tips about communication through iPads and technology.

"The ages of 12-18 are fundamental years for any person because that's when you learn life skills," says Kessia. "The mentoring program encourages us to get out and be involved."

Many doors have been opened for Kessia through Mizizi Maji. As a Junior Advocate for Girls Growing II Women, a program developed by Mizizi Maji intern Latasha Robertson-Crump, Kessia offers guidance to young girls, assists in event planning and provides input for future discussion topics. Through Mizizi Maji, Kessia also learned about the LEAD program (Leadership, Employment, Achievement and Direction), a component of Grand Rapids Mayor George Heartwell's Youth Council. Kessia and other young people ages 15-21 received training in leadership, employability and computer skills. "LEAD teaches teens that it's important to be part of a community," says Kessia, "and encourages them to take opportunities that will lead to meaningful jobs." After completing the program she landed a job as an usher at DeVos Place. Kessia is also currently involved in planning the HIV/AIDS Teen Summit "I'm Not About That Life," an educational forum that encourages positive self esteem, teaches young people to cultivate healthy relationships and motivates them to avoid at-risk behaviors.

For students in the Mizizi Maji program, one-to-one mentor matches are gradual and born out of relationships developed during weekly group mentoring meetings. Some students seek one-to-one mentoring, others seek group mentoring and others are interested in both. Kessia was matched with her mentor, Danielle, in 2012, and their relationship is evidenced by mutual trust and respect. Whether on a rock climbing adventure or a college visit to the University of Michigan, Kessia knows she can trust Danielle to offer a listening ear and a helping hand.

Today Kessia, a poised and confident 17-year-old, is President of Mizizi Maji. She regularly meets with Miss Sharon to provide a student's perspective about upcoming events and takes part in running weekly meetings. As a senior at East Kentwood, Kessia realizes the responsibility of being a role model. "I'm in the position now where younger students are asking me questions," she says. "If I could do a commercial for the program, I would say to kids: 'If you invest in material things, those things will wear out and have to be replaced, but the things you learn from Mizizi Maji experiences and trips will last a lifetime!'"

Latasha Robertson-Crump and Sandy Robertson
Mizizi Maji Mentors

Sandy Robertson recalls in the 1970s when her late father, Pastor Erskin Robertson of Friendship Missionary Baptist Church on Baxter Street in Grand Rapids, collaborated with the newly opened Baxter Community Center to meet the growing needs of the neighborhood. It was Sandy's daughter, Latasha Robertson-Crump, who encouraged her to become involved at Baxter decades later.

As an undergraduate at Kuyper College, Latasha interned in the Mizizi Maji Mentoring Program in 2012. She gained invaluable experience in event organization and conducted evidenced–based research on relevant topics. But it was her interactions with the young people, ages 8–18, which stoked her passion to serve.

"One of the benefits of the program is that it's a safe, warm place," says Latasha. "At meetings, kids talk about things that are important to them and ask their mentors things they might not feel comfortable bringing up at home. Most of our discussions, while not directly about self-esteem, build self-esteem and confidence. Education is a huge emphasis. Students know the better their grade point average is, the more opportunities they'll have, such as the 3.0 Gets To Go trips." While chaperoning one such trip to Chicago, Latasha as well learned more about her own history at the DuSable Museum of African American History.

Latasha was impressed with the reciprocal giving evidenced at Baxter. Many parents whose children benefit from the program give back by volunteering in Baxter's other pillars, such as the Threads sewing group and Marketplace. Others are Mizizi Maji volunteer mentors. These parents and other community members shape the lives and characters of young people by attending weekly meetings and providing either group or one-to-one mentoring; they also provide transportation, assist with special events and chaperone on extended trips. Latasha had benefited from a strong, loving family herself, and she encouraged her mom, Sandy, to become a mentor.

"A lot of people are inspired to give back when something has affected them," explains Sandy, "but I was raised by two wonderful parents and never had to struggle. I've seen how life-changing this program is for kids, and giving back has also been life-changing for me. Kids need a strong support system, but some of them have challenges that I never knew. Now that I see the need, serving has become a passion for me. And the fact that Mizizi Maji is a Christian program is evident in all they do.

"After I was at Baxter for a while as a group mentor," Sandy continues, "Ms. Sharon LaChappelle (Program Director) got a vibe that I was connecting with one particular 16-year-old young lady and asked if I would consider being her one-to-one mentor. At first I was hesitant–I knew it would be a big time commitment and I had already raised a teenager. But I agreed, and my parenting experience kicked in."

Sandy has gone above and beyond in her role as mentor. Not only does she take her mentee to dinner and movies, she also became an educational advocate when the girl's needs were not being met at school. "She is smart and has so much potential," explains Sandy, "but we needed to get her where she deserves to be." After making dozens of phone calls and learning the system, Sandy lined up a private tutor for her mentee from Aquinas College. Jubilee Jobs provided a summer opportunity for the young woman at the Seidman Center.

Along with job assistance, mentoring program students who need an academic boost throughout the school year may come to Baxter for free tutoring on Tuesdays and Thursdays. "The students gain so much," says Sandy, "but they are held to a higher standard. Community service is part of the program, so they learn it's important to give back." Students volunteer at Kids' Food Basket and at the neighborhood cleanup day.

So inspired was Latasha during her Baxter internship, she continued to volunteer after it ended. She collaborated with Dr. Dianne Green-Smith from Grand Valley State University and other Baxter members to organize local Teen Summit events and decided to pursue her Masters in Social Work at Grand Valley State University. Latasha put her knowledge to use by starting her own organization, Girls Growing II Women, which also meets at Baxter Community Center.

"I always wanted to organize a group to help people," says Latasha, "and the internship made me realize that my passion was for young ladies. The purpose of Girls Growing II Women is to prepare young women ages 13–21 for their futures." Latasha and another impassioned young woman, Jennifer Robertson, lead workshops twice a month to teach life skills and engage the group in discussions about relationships.

"We talk about relationships with boys, family and friends." says Latasha. "We have discussions about Facebook etiquette, sexual health and self esteem. This is a prevention group; there many groups for troubled kids, but it's our goal to impact girls so they never get to that point."

Sandy is understandably proud of her daughter and supports her every step of the way. "It takes a village," she says. "We are all striving for the same goals–happiness and prosperity–and the Mizizi Maji program makes it happen for a lot of kids."

Loutisha Patterson
Prayer Clinic

Prayer has always been the keystone in Loutisha "Tish" Patterson's life. Throughout her marriage to Virgil Patterson, the first ordained African American pastor in the Christian Reformed Church, the couple spent time together asking God's blessings upon their family and community. Racial tensions that escalated in the 1960s lingered throughout subsequent decades. When Baxter Community Center opened in the late '60s, it was a safe haven for neighbors and a place to go for food and clothing.

Seeds were planted early for Baxter's growth and expansion. "My husband and I prayed regularly for Baxter Community Center," says Tish. "Virgil had a vision that Baxter would fill the gaps, including a full medical clinic."

Virgil was spiritual advisor to Rosie Saverson-Hair, who, in one of the darkest seasons of her life, prayed that God would provide a job for her. She considered it a miracle when, in the late '70s, she was hired by Baxter as a counselor. In her new position, Rosie helped community members work through deep emotional needs; she also heard of many health issues that were not being addressed because of lack of insurance and income. Along with the Pattersons and other Baxter staff members, Rosie prayed for three years that God would provide a way for Baxter to meet these needs.

"Rosie attended a conference," says Tish, "where she met Dr. Bob Bulten and his wife, Ina, a nurse. When the Bultens mentioned they were looking for volunteer opportunities, Rosie 'captured' them." Soon other doctors and nurses from Dr. Bulten's practice, Alger Pediatrics, were also volunteering weekly at Baxter. The medical and dental clinics continued to grow into a truly wholistic practice, serving mind, body and spirit. What began as a well-baby facility extended to meet the needs of generations and the broader community.

Virgil passed away in 1982, and the next year Tish began volunteering at Baxter. She had always known that Baxter was Christ-centered, but as a volunteer she saw it firsthand. "Before the clinic opens," she says, "the doctors and nurses join hands to pray for the people they serve." As Tish and Ina Bulten worked side by side, they were moved to start a support group for mothers in the community. "Most of the moms were single," says Tish. "We studied the Bible and talked about the challenges they faced while raising children on limited incomes."

Tish joined Baxter's staff as Community Outreach Coordinator, providing intake services for clinic patients. "I asked them what they needed from the clinic," says Tish, "and sometimes they asked for prayer. I'd pray with them, and staff prayed for these individual needs as well." In her new role, Tish discovered that, while Baxter neighbors' needs spanned the medical spectrum, they had many things in common. "There are so many challenges when families have limited income," she says, "but they have the same needs and desires as everyone else: they want what's best for their children. We're all the same on that level."

When Tish was 65, she began to pray about her future. "I asked the Lord when I should retire," she says, "and He told me to work for three more years. After I retired in 2001 I asked God to show me what He wanted me to be doing. I remember having a dream about people coming to my door. I realized I was to be an intercessor in prayer for

people at Baxter. Because of the work that goes on there, the staff needs to be covered in prayer. They have a lot of challenges, and some people are not always accepting."

Tish and her prayer partner, Mary Cancler, have placed prayer request boxes in the various Baxter departments to allow clients and staff to submit specific requests. Tish and Mary pray daily for these individual needs and for Baxter's four pillars (Marketplace, the Mizizi Maji Mentoring Program, the Child Development Center and the Wholistic Health Clinic), including staff and volunteers. They also pray for Jubilee Jobs, located in Baxter's building, a nonprofit organization that provides employment readiness training and job opportunities for the economically underserved.

"I have learned not to judge people by the way they come across," says Tish. "Sometimes people seem harsh, but a lot of times it's because of the situations they are in and the hurts they are experiencing. Sometimes they feel hopeless, that nobody cares, so it's important to accept them and take the time to listen.

"Baxter staff are here because they want to be here," Tish continues. "The doctors and nurses are compassionate Christians and believe in Baxter's mission. They accept everyone without judgment. When people are cared for and prayed over, they feel safe and have trust. One time a young man came to the clinic for services. He was on probation and needed to be someplace, but he didn't have the money to get there so he was scared. We were praying for him. A doctor from the clinic took money from her own purse and gave it to him."

Baxter's medical and dental staff continually goes above and beyond for their patients. While the benefits of prayer cannot be measured with statistics, charts or graphs, it is prayer that makes the Baxter clinic community unique. "We value relationships," says Tish. "I always say we are a family."

Quentin Patterson
Child Development Center

If you pick up the thread of Quentin Patterson's story, it cannot be separated from the tapestry of Baxter Community Center's interwoven relationships. The care extended to one family member impacts generations, which in turn strengthens the broader community.

Quentin's grandparents, Virgil and Tish Patterson, prayed faithfully for Baxter since its inception in the 1960s. After Tish joined the Baxter staff, relationships deepened through shared experiences and communal prayer. Among those who joined her in prayer were Counselor Rosie Saverson-Hair, Child Development Center Director Ollie Lacy, Volunteer Pediatrician Dr. Ron Hofman and Adult Clinic Nurse Lori Eizenga.

"I joined Baxter in 1992," says Lori. "The staff prayed for clients and for each other. I got to know Tish, and we prayed for her daughter Sophia, a single mom with three young children." When Sophia was murdered in 1996, Quentin's half sister and half brother went to live with their fathers. Since Quentin's father hadn't been part of his life, a distant relative became his guardian. Tish picked Quentin up every week to attend worship services and Sunday School at Neland Christian Reformed Church.

"Every Sunday, like clockwork, I could count on Grandma," says Quentin, now 22. "She knew my mom would have wanted her kids to know each other, so she took us to the park and out to eat. She taught me about God, and she always prayed that He would protect me."

It was Tish's habit to pray aloud while she drove Quentin back to his guardian. "Sometimes I would forget," says Tish, "and Quentin would say, 'Granny, you forgot to pray!' " After Quentin's guardian became abusive, Tish took him into her home. "Because Quentin was so active and needed more than I could give," she says, "I prayed for a Christian mother and father. The clinic staff prayed as well." While Tish was working, Quentin was enrolled in Baxter's Child Development Center. "Ms. Lacy was so good for Quentin," says Tish. "Because of all he'd been through, sometimes he'd have outbursts of anger. Later he'd come back and say he was sorry."

Dr. Hofman and his wife, Heidi, took Quentin into their home on weekends. "The people at Baxter helped me heal and shaped my character," says Quentin. "The abuse took a toll, so Rosie recommended a counselor who helped me, but I was still scared. I felt like I never fit in."

Baxter staff continued to pray that God would provide parents for Quentin. Lori Eizenga also prayed for Quentin on her own. She recalls the day, while vacuuming her living room, when she clearly heard God ask, "Why not you?"

"I'd never had an experience like that before," says Lori. "It was shocking because I'd never considered adopting Quentin. Our son Nate was 14 and Jordan was 11; my husband Doug and I hadn't planned to expand our family. I asked Rosie to pray for direction. After a lot of soul searching and prayer, Doug and I believed we were called to adopt Quentin. We approached Tish with our offer and said that maybe we weren't what she had in mind, since we were Dutch, white and middle-class."

"When Lori approached me," says Tish, "I said, 'I don't remember asking God for parents of a specific color.'"

"From the time I heard God's voice," says Lori, "to the time Quentin joined our family was exactly nine months. It was like a spiritual pregnancy, a time for us to get ready to take him into our home."

"Having mother and father figures," says Quentin, "was a challenge. I was rebellious because I didn't know how to respond."

"The adjustment was hard," Lori acknowledges, "but Quentin had surprisingly little damage to his soul; he never believed he deserved his experiences. I think of it as a way God protected him, which made it possible for him to heal."

In her fifteen years at Baxter, Lori drew on established relationships. "My African American sisters," she says, "taught me how to raise an African American boy. It was important to help Quentin be comfortable with who he was and yet feel he was part of our family, too. Having Quentin in our family expanded our horizons. He had the energy to play every sport, and he did it all well. He's very open, and he's caused us to grow and be more open, too." During the summers while Lori worked, Quentin spent his days in Baxter's Child Development Center, and he continued as Dr. Hofman's patient until he graduated from high school.

"I wouldn't wish what happened to me on anyone, "says Quentin, "but I do wish the lessons upon people. I believe you grow more through pain than when times are easy. If things happen to you when you're younger, it breaks you, and you have to figure out a way to overcome obstacles. My counselors taught me to be a conqueror, not a victim; through this mindset I can reach a lot of people."

As a Youth Treatment Specialist at Wedgwood Christian Services, Quentin helps residents work through issues. "I help clients get to a level of trust," says Quentin. "Sometimes their greatest fear is getting close to someone. Exposure to so many people keeps me from having barriers; instead of noticing a person's color, I see their potential and give them the benefit of the doubt. Being a part Baxter was a demonstration of how people should treat each other, and that will always stay with me."

Ms. Ollie Lacy
Child Development Center

"I always say God has a way of placing you where He wants you," says Ollie Lacy. "And I'm grateful He placed me at Baxter."

"Ms. Lacy" was hired as a teacher in Baxter's Child Development Center (CDC) in 1980. When she became the program's director two years later, she had two goals. "I wanted people to know," she says, "that the Baxter CDC was a quality inner city program." The CDC has been nationally accredited since 2007, a distinction held by less than 5% of Kent County childcare programs.

"My other goal," says Ms. Lacy, "was to expand our hours so parents would have a place for their children while they worked. Neighborhood kids were going home to empty houses after school." An infant program was added in 2000, and the CDC provided before- and after-school care for students. "Kids put on plays, learned to sew, learned about other countries–and we made it fun," Ms. Lacy recalls. A summer program provided rich learning opportunities and field trips.

Ms. Lacy soon noticed another age group that needed care. "I'd look out the window and see teens loitering, with nothing productive to do. Sometimes the staff would break up fights, bring kids in and ask what we could do. They'd say they were bored and felt nobody cared. Many had only one parent. Any help they got at school stopped at a certain age. Kids lose people in their lives; we had to figure out what to do for them. They needed structure and someone to tell them they're important."

An answer came to Ms. Lacy in the form of a dream one night: kids needed mentors who would walk alongside their families, even when they reached adulthood. The dream turned into a shared vision, and Baxter's Mizizi Maji Mentoring Program was born. "Some kids went from the CDC to the mentoring program," says Ms. Lacy, "and those connections last a lifetime."

Ms. Lacy knew the importance of intergenerational relationships; for the past decade, CDC students have visited monthly with Fulton Manor seniors for projects and activities. "Sometimes, when kids see older people struggle with walking or talking, or with an oxygen tank, they're scared," says Ms. Lacy. "When kids spend time with seniors they're not afraid, and everybody benefits."

Local philanthropists have had continuing relationships with the CDC. "The kids sang at Peter Cook's 50th birthday celebration," recalls Ms. Lacy. "We built a bird feeder for Peter Wege's birthday one year. Fred Meijer stopped by out of the blue to drop off a new television set. And one year we wrote our own song and performed it at an event honoring Rich DeVos.

Today, the CDC serves a diverse population; families represent many cultures, religions and economic backgrounds. The CDC partners with the Early Learning Neighborhood Collaborative to provide a kindergarten-readiness classroom. Scholarships allow 16 preschoolers to attend for free. Other CDC programs operate on a sliding scale fee structure based on household income. Baxter cares about the well being of each child's family. Parents can benefit from Baxter's Marketplace, and family members can receive services from Baxter's Wholistic Health Clinic.

Baxter teachers are intentional about each child's social, spiritual, emotional and academic needs. All CDC classrooms have an interest-led approach to learning and use the accredited *Creative Curriculum.* One year, when neighborhood streets were being torn up and repaved, kids were enthralled as they watched the progress, so art projects and activities centered on construction equipment and tools. Students learn how to plant and harvest in Baxter's Greenhouse. Preschoolers create projects for CDC's in-house ArtPrize and benefit from lessons conducted by the Grand Rapids Public Museum. Field trips include excursions to Frederik Meijer Gardens, local orchards, libraries and John Ball Zoo.

The CDC benefits from numerous collaborations. An instructor from YMCA's "Two Peas in a Pod" program gives a weekly nutrition lesson and brings healthy snacks. Volunteers from Calvin College, Aquinas College and Grand Valley State University read to children, organize and clean, and help assemble promotional materials. Jenison Christian School students and church youth groups help out during service projects. For the past 20 years, Comerica Bank has purchased Christmas gifts for CDC kids. The Kent County Medical Society Alliance asks for a supply wish list each year and responds generously, along with hosting a Christmas party in December. Seniors from the Gerontology Network volunteer in preschool classrooms and rock babies to sleep in the nursery; one woman, Grandma Barb, faithfully answers the phone and opens the door for children each morning.

"Baxter is so important to the neighborhood," says Ms. Lacy. "It's my wish for people to see that contributing their time, even an hour a week rocking a baby, is important. Every financial contribution helps."

At Ms. Lacy's retirement in 2011 it was said that she 'had a way of encouraging children that seemed to spread to everyone else. When kids needed comfort, they got it by seeing her face.'

"Sometimes there was deep sadness in kids' eyes," says Ms. Lacy, "but they knew that even when tragedies happen, we still have each other. Baxter has been there for me, too, during difficult times. When you're a part of a community for so long, it gets to be your family."

Catherine's
HEALTH CENTER

Mission: *Catherine's Health Center provides high quality, affordable and compassionate health care to the underserved in our neighborhood.*

1211 Lafayette Ave NE
Grand Rapids, MI 49505
616.336.8800
catherineshc.org

–Catherine's Health Center–

Roots

When vulnerable groups lack access to resources the entire community suffers. Working poor or simply poor people endure health challenges and risk devastating complications when health care access is limited. With that conviction and a context of scarce family medical resources in northeast Grand Rapids, concerned activists, people of faith and a major health care provider met in 1993 to improvise a solution. Adding urgency, the local Health Department Well Child Clinic was to close.

The result was "Catherine's Care Center." Unveiled in 1996, the drop-in clinic was housed in the basement of St. Alphonsus Parish, largely funded through St. Mary's Hospital and shaped by Creston Neighborhood Association leadership. Near the corner of Leonard and Lafayette, it was adjacent to a city bus stop and served the Creston and Belknap neighborhoods.

The name references Catherine McAuley, an Irish heiress who directed her considerable fortune to serving poor, homeless women and children of Dublin, Ireland, with a home and education. In 1831 McAuley founded the Sisters of Mercy, which, in 1893 established St. Mary's Hospital in Grand Rapids.

Catherine's primary service population is two neighborhoods with combined populations of 30,000. Diversity, zones in transition, and significant numbers of under-served people characterize the target area. Around 8% of the Creston neighborhood and 27% of the Belknap population lives at or below the federal poverty level. Educational achievement lags in the larger community; those employed often labor in entry level and service positions. About 70% of Catherine's patients live in its target neighborhoods. Honoring its commitment to serving people in challenging straits and noting there are few safety net providers, the Center's door is open to the broader community.

Steady Growth

Catherine's Care Center opened as a nurse-run clinic where children could receive immunizations, health education and free medical screenings. When families' additional unmet needs surfaced, service expansion allowed the nurse to address adult health issues, refer patients for immediate care and help families find providers.

In 2000 a doctor volunteer joined the nurse, enabling Catherine's to introduce free medical services two days per week. Still, dozens were turned away daily as the cramped church basement quarters and an insufficient number of providers limited capacity.

The response came in 2009 through the *Opening Doors Campaign.* The

$1.275 million goal would create the opportunity to re-purpose a vacant wing of the former St. Alphonsus School into an expanded clinic. Launched during an economic downturn when other campaigns were floundering, the effort was met by a generous community. Funds exceeded the goal, creating a modest margin to operate the expanded, renamed clinic. To reduce confusion, convey clearly the nature of the agency and retain reference to its namesake, the clinic was renamed "Catherine's Health Center."

With six times its former space, Catherine's remains a vital part of the health care safety net, completing more than 7,000 visits annually. Staff and volunteers serve the community in well-equipped exam rooms. Patients appreciate a spacious waiting room, and work stations truly support staff and volunteers as they make referrals, dispense medications and coordinate treatment. Clinical care, health education, lifestyle coaching and more are offered five days a week by a core staff of physicians, nurses and assistants. A small board leadership group provides direction, solicits funding and represents Catherine's in and beyond the community.

Today Catherine's offers medical care to community residents with income up to 250% of the federal poverty level. Many come from the ranks of the working poor. Some, holding down two or more subsistence level jobs but with limited resources, are faced with having to put food on the table rather than seek health care. When lacking money for  medications, they may defer or avoid care despite chronic conditions. Limited health information often shapes lifestyles and health practices, creating risk for health crises, loss of productivity and financial ruin.

LEED Gold Certified

Catherine's Health Center has modeled stewardship. When planning a new clinic, green building principles made sense. Generous support enabled the clinic to achieve Gold certification under the Leadership in Energy and Environmental Design (LEED) rating system, an internationally recognized benchmark for the design, construction and operation of "green" buildings. The Gold ranking certifies that the renovated facility successfully employs a variety of sustainable measures improving performance in areas of human and environmental health.

Re-purposing an existing building, recycling materials from St. Alphonsus School and purchasing low-impact, locally manufactured materials were among areas earning LEED points. The result is a clinic that operates efficiently and minimizes waste. Catherine's Health Center is proud to be the first safety net clinic in the Midwest, and one of only a handful in the country, to achieve this prestigious award.

*Optometry services brighten the days for Catherine's patients
thanks to gift support, volunteered professional time and expertise.*

Funding

From 1996 through the spring of 2005 Saint Mary's Hospital, Creston Neighborhood Association and St. Alphonsus Parish operated the Center through a Memorandum of Agreement. In 2005 re-prioritization of commitments led Saint Mary's to discontinue financial support, a potentially devastating blow to the busy clinic.

Despite loss of funding and management support, and with other challenges staring them down, the core of Catherine's leadership held firm, determined to see transition to an independent clinic that would maintain its commitment to the community. Their work was rewarded when a board was formed, the agency was incorporated and, in 2007, the IRS awarded nonprofit status, clearing the way for soliciting donated funds to sustain services.

Through challenging times, leadership honed skills in grant writing, fundraising, and financial management, work that brought considerable success and respect. Today 85% of the clinic's operating revenue comes from charitable gifts and grants while 15% comes through fees for services, primarily paid as a result of the few insurance products now available to some patients. With a view toward sustainability, Catherine's is intent on growing its endowment fund.

Partners

The clinic often describes its role as "your neighborhood working together for a healthier you." Catherine's works toward this ideal by collaborating

139

with other health agencies to bring patients the finest health care available. A partial listing of partners includes Advanced Radiology Services, AmeriCorps VISTA, Avon Foundation Breast Care Fund, AstraZeneca HealthCare Foundation, Blue Cross Blue Shield Foundation, Calvin College Nursing Department, Cook Charitable Foundation, Free Clinics of Michigan, Grand Rapids Community Foundation, Grand Rapids Public Schools, Health Intervention Services (HIS), Kent County Health Department, Kent Medical Foundation, Kirkhof School of Nursing at Grand Valley State University, Mercy Health Saint Mary's Health Care, Michigan Cancer Consortium, Michigan Consumers for Healthcare, Michigan Department of Community Health, Michigan State University College of Human Medicine, New City Urban Farms, Nokomis Foundation, Saint Alphonsus Parish, Spectrum Health, Sebastian Foundation, Steelcase Foundation, Susan G Komen West Michigan, Wege Foundation, YMCA and YWCA. Catherine's deeply values multiple individual, business, foundation, church and family donors whose generosity and support make our community stronger and healthier.

As those with limited or no medical insurance typically cannot afford medications, staff and volunteers help patients obtain prescription drugs. The Medication Assistance Program (MAP) at Catherine's operates out of dedicated space adjacent to the patient checkout station. Patients who need access to low or no-cost prescriptions simply stop at the MAP desk where a staff member confirms the medication is available through one of the pharmaceutical companies. Medication is ordered and the patient is instructed to return to Catherine's where it will be dispensed. Catherine's helps people access prescription medications with a total value well over a half million dollars every year. Patients also receive inexpensive and generic medications valued in the thousands of dollars through the clinic each month.

Beyond medical services, its collaborative nature has promoted development of many community-oriented services. Using medical staff, neighborhood volunteers, and AmeriCorps VISTA workers, Catherine's sponsors outreach activities including free educational health fairs, free pap smears and mammograms for eligible women, a community walking program, blood pressure, blood sugar, and cholesterol screening events and community influenza immunization events. Catherine's also maintains and values relationships with local colleges and universities to provide undergraduate students, Registered Nursing students, Physician Assistant and Nurse Practitioner students and medical students with education and training in a community health care setting.

Honors

In 2001, Catherine's Health Center received the first annual *Douglas A. Mack Award* from the Kent County Health Department for community collaboration and improving the health status of the community. In 2005 and 2008, the Michigan Peer Review Organization granted the *Governor's Award* for excellence in primary care services. In 2013 Catherine's received the *Torch Award* from the Better Business Bureau® Serving Western Michigan and the *Spirit of Collaboration Award* through the Michigan Cancer Consortium. In 2010 Karen Kaashoek, Executive Director of Catherine's, was recognized with a *YWCA of Grand Rapids Tribute Award* in connection with her work advancing the mission.

Vision

Catherine's core values are: social justice, service, dignity and stewardship. The organization' vision is to fulfill its mission so well that other communities are inspired to do likewise. This requires services that are:

- Safe: Avoid injuries to patients from the care that is intended to help them.
- Effective: Match care to science; avoid overuse of ineffective care and underuse of effective care.
- Patient-Centered: Honor the individual and respect his or her choices.
- Timely: Reduce waiting for both patients and those who give care.
- Equitable: Close racial and ethnic gaps in health status.
- Sustainable: Seek new resources and be an exceptional steward of those we have.
- Efficient: Reduce waste.

Open Doors—Catherine's exists to improve access for those in need of health care services. This may include assistance in accessing solutions within the broader health care delivery system.

Quality Care—Catherine's believes everyone deserves to have their health care needs met in a caring and dignified manner. Dedicated staff and volunteers strive to make Catherine's a medical home for our patients.

The success of Catherine's Health Center can be attributed to committed staff, volunteers and donors who embrace the mission. They live up to the words of the clinic's namesake, Venerable Sister Catherine McAuley: "We should be as shining lamps, giving light to all around us."

Sharon Esterley
Patient

"I'm an angel person," says Sharon Esterley when asked about the pin she wears that features the image of an angel centered in a heart. "I believe in angels and have lots of them in my life looking after me. Some are from my church, St. Paul's United Methodist, some are from Catherine's Health Center and others are from various friends."

For the past three years Sharon has relied on Catherine's Health Center for her primary medical care. "First Dr. Jack and now Dr. Jon— they're great!" she enthuses, adding that she's had good experiences with everyone she's met at the Center.

Raised in Kentwood, Sharon worked for 32 years as a nurses' aid. When her aging parents needed help, she quit work to become their caregiver, an arrangement that lasted for nine years until they both passed away. She then became the primary caregiver for a close friend. During those years Sharon lacked health care coverage and, through the urging of a friend, began to receive medical care through Catherine's.

Sharon was able to fill her medications through Catherine's Medication Assistance Program, attend diabetes management classes and participate in the Community Walking Program. She worked with one of Catherine's Navigators (people trained to provide objective information on insurance options and help people access information and complete applications) to receive Medicaid coverage. While arthritis and a pre-diabetic condition were the focal points of her care, Sharon was essentially healthy and able to return to paid employment. At 59 years old, Sharon wanted to try something different after years of paid and family caregiving, and took work as a custodian with Goodwill Industries.

"Over the years, my back would act up from time to time," says Sharon, "but it was nothing serious. Then, in January of 2014, without warning, I collapsed with unbearable pain that started in my left leg and spread to my hip and back. The pain was excruciating."

Sharon was diagnosed with sciatica. The doctor felt that her many years of lifting patients as a caregiver was a major contributor to her condition. Although she was faithful to physical therapy sessions at Catherine's, she was still using a walker, not sleeping at night and generally feeling miserable and unable to complete the tasks required for work. Consequently, Catherine's referred her to Mary Free Bed Rehabilitation Center for more intensive physical therapy. Still Sharon's pain and distress didn't subside.

Looking for a new option, Sharon was seen by Dr. Jon Reitzenstein not long after his arrival at Catherine's. Trained in acupuncture, Dr. Jon believed some relief was possible through the administration of auriculotherapy–simply put, treatments involving key points in the outer ear that, when stimulated, provide relief from pain. Sharon was willing to try the technique and just as the doctor expected, the procedures were successful. After just two treatments Sharon noticed a substantial reduction in her pain, and after seven treatments, she says the pain is mostly gone. In addition, she went from using a wheelchair, to a walker, to a cane, and now walks completely unassisted. She is sleeping again and she uses no medication to manage her pain. The acupuncture treatments have been discontinued, although Dr. Jon plans to monitor Sharon's progress. "The day I walked into physical therapy on my own two legs, I cried from happiness," says Sharon. "I haven't taken a sleeping pill in many weeks and I'm sleeping all night."

"I thank God for Catherine's Health Center," Sharon continues. "People there have really helped me."

After recently completing a program at the Women's Resource Center to update her work skills and build her confidence, Sharon is back to the work she loves—that of being a caregiver—this time as a companion assistant for Elders' Helpers. "I have so many angels in my life; I want to be an angel for others, too," she beams.

Philadore Davids
Patient

Born the oldest of 18 children in Cape Town, South Africa, under the apartheid system, Philadore Davids's life has been challenging. (Apartheid was a system of legally-enforced racial segregation in South Africa from 1948-1994.)

"At four, I was carrying babies around," she says without complaint, noting that was simply a part of her family life. Although it wasn't always so, she now embraces her first name, which has Greek roots and translates to "love, love." She notes her grandmother's favorite cologne was so-named, an association she also now enjoys.

Philadore's life took a dark turn when she was only 17. Young, female, and of mixed racial heritage (she was identified as "coloured" in her native South Africa, which made her vulnerable to segregation and ethnic prejudice), Philadore had little voice and few options when she became pregnant after she was raped. No one believed the handsome, popular and outwardly desirable fellow had forced himself on her and, in keeping with the practice of the day, she was forced to marry the father of the child.

Her husband remained abusive and Philadore lost that first baby after a beating. She went on to have four more children with him, three sons and a daughter. She cherishes her children and grandchildren, but now, after 30 years on her own, does not miss the husband who abused her. In South Africa, she says, such matters were considered a domestic problem with no call for outside intervention.

Philadore considers herself independent, determined and strong of character. A born salesperson, she held a position working trade shows and took pride in representing quality products with integrity. "I was very good at it," she says. Yet life has challenged her. With help from one of her sons, she relocated to the United States around 2010 and lived with his family. Eventually she needed a place of her own but her options were limited due to her depleted resources. A combination of circumstances eroded Philadore's savings, left her without a car, and put her in a precarious private employment situation which collapsed after an extended period of work without pay.

"I trust the Lord," she says, but admits that even people of faith lose heart at times. A case of meningitis put her in need of medical care and she found her way to Catherine's about 2011. "Dr. Jack is an angel," says Philadore, "a kind and caring doctor. He, Mark Contreras, R.N., and everyone at Catherine's has been wonderful to me," she says.

The meningitis was successfully treated with an eight-day hospital stay, for which she is grateful. Carpal tunnel syndrome, foot pain, vertigo and a depressed mood followed in the wake of further losses, and Philadore again needed help, a difficult thing for an independent person to accept, she says.

Now Philadore is benefitting from acupuncture treatments offered by the clinic's Dr. Jon. "It's given me wonderful relief from the pain in my wrists and body," she says, noting that her pain level has dropped from a 10 to a 2. Along with the pain relief she is experiencing an improvement in her mood. She attributes the pain to muscle stress and strain from  her work as a caregiver, cooking and cleaning in an adult foster care home for women with a history of behavioral health issues. She professes love for the women she cares for, even though the physical demands of caregiving 24/7 haven't been kind to her 66-year-old body.

Philadore likes to work and doesn't want to be dependent on the government. "I came here for a better life, not to sit on my bum and take handouts," she says.

Through it all, Philadore can't say enough about the help she's received through Catherine's, especially the pain relief she's experienced through auriculotherapy, acupuncture treatments administered at the outer ear. "My painful, swollen wrists are so much better now. I am so relieved. It's interesting that I got so much help from the needles," she says with a laugh, referring to the small acupuncture needles used in her treatments. "I prefer the acupuncture to medications," Philadore continues, "and am amazed at how well it works. I'm recommending it to so many people. You gotta keep an open mind and believe in it. It's worked for me."

Moody Firth
Patient

"I've been going to Catherine's for years," says Moody Firth. "I remember when I used to see Dr. Jack in the basement of the church." Moody is referring to St. Alphonsus Church, the location of Catherine's Health Center's from 1996-2011.

A transplant from a small town situated along the east coast near Newport News, Virginia, Moody describes his family as being involved in the seafood industry. "That's how they all make their living—from seafood. I love Southern food," he says with a smile, but goes on to say that the diet caught up with him. "I needed a doctor but I had no money, no insurance and no place to go. My daughter found Catherine's and that's how I got started."

Moody Firth works with a navigator from Catherine's to apply for health insurance.

Moody confirms that at the first visit his blood pressure, cholesterol and blood sugar level were all elevated, due in part perhaps, to his diet. "Dr. Jack helped me out a lot," he says. "Now I manage my diabetes, and my blood pressure and cholesterol are down." Moody gives himself insulin injections twice daily, which he gets through Catherine's MAP (Medical Assistance Program). He has an appointment at the Health Center every three months to monitor his levels, at which time Dr. Jack keeps him in line regarding the management of his health. Through Dr. Jack and Catherine's nutritionist, Moody has learned that much of the Southern food he so enjoyed did his body no favors and consequently, he has since changed his eating habits.

"I no longer eat fried foods," says Moody. "Plus I now make better choices, like eating whole wheat bread instead of white bread." Moody and his wife Cindy share cooking preparation and both have benefitted from healthier eating.

Recently retired, Moody first came to Michigan around 1971 to find work. He left for a time but returned to the Grand Rapids area 36 years ago, and with his four children and six grandchildren nearby, he sees himself staying. During the construction season, Moody ran the paver for an asphalt company. "Thirty-five years in that work is long enough," he says. His income varied by the season, leaving him without medical benefits. Now Moody is working with one of Catherine's navigators to learn about insurance coverage options that may help him. He's not sure yet whether he will qualify or what choices he may have, but he hopes the day is soon coming when he won't receive so many calls from telemarketers offering insurance coverage.

Catherine's proved to be a great fit for Moody. "The people are all real good here," he says, adding that everyone, but especially Dr. Jack, has been helpful to him. "Everybody I interact with is friendly and helpful," continues Moody. "You can't ask for better people. If it wasn't for them, I don't know where I'd be, what I would do. I know lots of other people depend on them, too."

When asked if he would be willing to share his story, Moody immediately said, "Sure, whatever I can do to help!" He's a great example of the hard-working folks with limited health care resources that Catherine's helps. Now he hopes that sharing his story will inspire others.

Ellie Burke
Patient

As a 22-year-old part-time fitness instructor without health insurance, Ellie Burke knew she needed medical care when she developed a severe respiratory infection. With the help of a friend, Ellie made an appointment at Catherine's Health Center. That was in 2004, and over the next decade Ellie continued to use the health clinic for her annual checkups and occasional illnesses.

At one point, Ellie's assigned physician, Dr. John Walen, suspected an enlarged liver based on manual examination, though her blood work did not indicate a problem. The condition is not uncommon. Still, while little evidence supported further immediate testing, the decision was to take a watchful approach while looking for resources to investigate more aggressively.

But in December 2013 Ellie was in pain. "The enlargement was pushing into my ribs and hurt a great deal," she says. "I have a twisted rib cage, so that was always a factor, too. I was quite uncomfortable and called Catherine's Health Center for an appointment."

"Dr. Walen took one look at me," says Ellie, "pressed on my stomach, and recommended an immediate CAT scan. I could tell he and Mark Contreras, the nurse, were very concerned, although they were trying hard to hide their thoughts. They were both very sweet and kind to me."

Catherine's scheduled an immediate CAT scan for Ellie at Spectrum Hospital and at 10:00 a.m. the morning after the diagnostic test, Dr. Walen called Ellie with the results. "Dr. Walen is a straight shooter," says Ellie, "which I appreciate. He told me there was a large mass on my kidney, not my liver. He had already called Spectrum and made an appointment for me with the urologic-oncology division.

"Dr. Walen went into the office on his day off and called me with the results so I wouldn't spend the weekend worrying," Ellie continues. "He also gave me his home phone number, because he knew that, as I processed the fact that I had kidney cancer, I would have questions. He said to call him anytime and he would do whatever he could to help me. What doctor does that?"

Ellie's tumor—larger than a cantaloupe—was successful removed by Dr. Brian Lane at Spectrum. As she recovered, Catherine's nurse Mark Contreras called Ellie to check on her condition and her post-operative MRI results. "Dr. Walen and Mark cared so much and were so considerate of me," says Ellie. "I was very touched." Luckily, Ellie did not need chemotherapy or radiation, but she will have periodic checkups and MRIs to monitor any possible future growths.

As a result of her positive experience with Catherine's, Ellie applied for a position at Spectrum. She has been working there the past few months, registering patients. She's also gone back to school to become a nurse. "All their help and care was inspiring," says Ellie. "I would never have considered going back to school and entering the health field if it hadn't been for this experience and the caring people at Catherine's. I want to give back by becoming a nurse myself."

Health care benefits come with Ellie's position at the hospital. "I am proud that I no longer need to depend on the goodness of Catherine's," says Ellie, "but I will never forget their treatment of me. They served me with respect and dignity and that meant the world to me. It's reassuring and heart-warming to know there's a place for people without insurance to have their medical needs met.

"I would have been lost without Catherine's over the past ten years," continues Ellie. "There are so many good people there, many of whom are volunteers, people who just want to help other people. It's very inspiring. It's changed my life."

Laura Bartlett
Patient

While some would envy her slight, petite build, Laura Bartlett says her body is just too small to tolerate some of the medications she hoped would provide relief from her anxiety. "Xanax, Wellbutrin—I really don't like those meds," she says. "Why would I put something in my body that doesn't help me feel good?" Still, Laura has resorted to strong medications in the past to cope with the stress symptoms she experiences.

Born in Bay City, Michigan, Laura had a difficult childhood and was 22 when she fled with her three-year-old daughter to New York after her abusive husband was jailed. She knew no one there; she was simply frightened, yet determined to escape the violence that left her with a broken jaw and other injuries. At first Laura relied on welfare. Later she found work with Verizon, eventually rising to become a senior administrative assistant. Returning to Michigan to follow her daughter about 15 years ago, Laura took an early retirement from Verizon.

It took a long time for Laura's hope for similar work in Michigan to materialize. She worked as a waitress but lost that job when she accompanied her significant other, Victor, as he drove a semi-truck cross country. "It's been a bad period," Laura says, as she offers a list of losses: when Victor fell behind on child support payments, New York courts seized his cash assets; the couple lost their apartment and became homeless; and Victor awaited back surgery. As a result, Laura became highly nervous and anxious. "I couldn't think straight," says Laura. "My chest was thumping. I knew I had to calm down."

Laura has been seeing Dr. Jon every other week for the past six months at Catherine's Health Center. She first met him in another clinic and felt she could trust him. "Dr. Jon knew I didn't want to rely on drugs for my symptoms," she says. "He's a good listener and doesn't judge me. He has faith in me." Laura goes on to describe a friend from New York, an adamant believer in alternative approaches to health. So, while Laura had never experienced acupuncture, she found herself open to it when Dr. Jon suggested it was likely to provide some relief from her anxiety and pain.

"For each treatment," says Laura, "I lie still while Dr. Jon inserts needles in my feet, the webbing between my thumbs and forefingers, and between my eyebrows." The locations of the needles may vary. Then Dr. Jon turns out the lights and Laura relaxes for five to ten minutes before he returns and removes the needles. Sometimes he inserts pins that stay in her earlobes for five days that Laura activates with a magnet.

"It's working," she smiles. "I feel better for a week after a treatment; that's a lot longer than with medication." Laura goes on to say that her head feels clearer and she's able to think and recall much better than before the treatments. "During a recent treatment I experienced two spasms as my muscles and nerves relaxed," says Laura. "It was remarkable and somewhat frightening. Dr. Jon said it was a sign that my tension was releasing."

Laura is feeling the best she ever has and thinks she and Dr. Jon are close to getting to the root of her anxiety, which feels like a fist pushing into the middle of her ribcage. No one has ever unraveled that "ball" of tension, but the acupuncture coupled with the anti-anxiety drug Buspar, which Dr. Jon prescribed, has eased her stress.

Laura is also currently troubled by a wire in her mouth, a leftover reminder of her fractured jaw and the subsequent surgical procedure to stabilize it almost thirty years ago. With her anxiety currently under control, Laura thinks she will be able to go through with the procedure, scheduled with an eye, ear, nose and throat specialist. "My dental work is almost complete now," says Laura, pleased that she has been able to take advantage of the Affordable Care Act to meet her medical, vision and dental needs.

Laura freely admits that her experiences over the years are the root of her anxiety and that they color her expectations and shape her hopes. Disappointments, hurts and fear have been her companions for a long while. Still, she enjoys feeling relief from anxiety after the acupuncture treatments and is very pleased to be less reliant on medications; she feels empowered by the results of the alternative treatment. Laura recently found work leasing housing units for a local property owner and hopes to do well in that position. She's excited to have connected recently with long-lost family members and retains her dream to someday own a mobile home.

Family Promise
of Grand Rapids
ending homelessness...one family at a time

Mission: Ending homelessness, one family at a time, by engaging community and faith-based organizations to provide emergency shelter and basic needs to families with children who are homeless and to provide additional programs to assist them in finding housing and sustaining their independence

906 South Division, Suite 205
Grand Rapids, MI 49507
616.475.5220
FamilyPromiseGR.org

–Family Promise of Grand Rapids–

Roots

In 1996 East Congregational United Church of Christ members were feeling lackluster about their community outreach. They began to search for a hands-on ministry that would involve a large number of congregants and also make use of their abundant, unused church space. Newly arrived pastor Brian Byrne suggested Interfaith Hospitality Network, a program his previous church members had embraced in Indianapolis. With the full support of his church's Board of Mission and Community Outreach, enthusiastic volunteers led by member Mary Ann March and commitments from eight other local congregations, Brian led the way to founding the Greater Grand Rapids Interfaith Hospitality Network (GGRIHN).

The national IHN program was begun a decade earlier by Karen Olson of Summit, New Jersey. When Karen and her son commuted into New York City for work each day, she saw homeless people on the street and in the bus station. One day she offered a sandwich to a woman and, in gratitude, the woman took Karen's hand. Karen sat down, had a conversation with the woman and learned her story. From that encounter Karen realized that "homeless people have hopes and dreams like you and me," she said. The incident inspired Karen to found IHN as a way to provide homeless families with temporary shelter.

In Grand Rapids, Brian Byrne, Mary Ann March and their committee worked diligently to get the program up and running in less than a year. A part-time executive director was hired, and twelve other congregations were recruited to provide overnight accommodations and support to the families. A Day Center was opened from 7:00 a.m. to 5:00 p.m. to provide a home base and the resources needed to search for employment and housing. In 2003 the national organization changed its name to "Family Promise" to reflect a broader range of programs and reaffirm its commitment to help families realize their own potential. Four years later the local Day Center moved to its current location at 906 South Division.

The recession in 2008 took a toll on families, and since then Family Promise has seen a significant rise in the need for

A host congregation member feeds a guest's baby

shelter, housing and basic needs for families with children. In response, Family Promise began to grow its focus on housing and aftercare supports to help families shorten or eliminate their need for shelter, decrease their recidivism back into homelessness and achieve a stable and healthy environment for their children. At that time the nonprofit's name officially changed to "Family Promise of Grand Rapids," following the name change of the national organization to account for the expansion of services beyond the original IHN shelter concept. It is one of 188 affiliates in 41 states.

Statistics tell some of the local story: since its inception in 1997, Family Promise of Grand Rapids has served over 2,000 children and 1,000 families through its programs and has provided 50% of the total capacity in Kent County for families to remain together when homeless. About 90% of Family Promise's families are successful in leaving shelter to find a new home, and more than 85% remain housed a year later.

Programs
To achieve its goal of providing children and their families with shelter, basic needs and assistance as they seek permanent housing, Family Promise partners with local congregations, individuals, families, foundations and corporations. It also encourages families to create an achievable vision and develop a strong foundation for self-sufficiency. The agency reaches this goal through four programs: *Interfaith Hospitality Network*, *Partners in Housing*, *Reaching Beyond Initiative* and their *Aftercare* Program.

Interfaith Hospitality Network—When a family is homeless and seeks to change their circumstances, Family Promise first provides emergency, temporary shelter through its *Interfaith Hospitality Network*. Families are housed overnight in one of its many host congregations. It is unique in that it does not split up families during their crisis; dads and boys over the age of 10 are allowed to remain with their families, keeping the family unit strong. Volunteers make meals for the families, sleep overnight at the church with them, play and read books to children and encourage interaction with their own families.

Families spend the day at Family Promise's Day Center, where they take advantage of its computer center, case managers and mentors to look for employment and housing. Volunteers also read to children, edit resumes and help families move. Children attend school. Every family is connected to the community through volunteers at the congregations, which allows them to build a new network that helps them achieve their goal of independence.

Partners in Housing—With a shortfall of affordable housing in the community, there's a real need to supply permanent housing for families who are homeless or at imminent risk of becoming homeless. For as little as $7,000, *Partners in Housing* restores manufactured homes so they become affordable places where families can be proud to live. When a family shows fiscal responsibility by consistently paying their rent and utilities and completes the program, they receive the title to their home. This opportunity takes a family out of homelessness into homeownership in as little as nine months. Family Promise currently works with manufactured home parks located in several communities in the greater Grand Rapids area.

Volunteers are utilized at this stage to clean a home before a family moves in. They install carpet and appliances, perform minor home repairs, paint, set up and arrange furniture, landscape, help families move, make lunch on move-in day, watch kids during the move and mentor a family. This program, with 50 homes completed since its inception in 2009, has been incredibly successful with 99% of the families still housed in their home or having moved on to permanent homes.

Reaching Beyond Initiative—This program provides emergency housing and basic needs support to families experiencing a housing crisis. In partnership with the local Coalition to End Homelessness, Family Promise provides shelter and basic needs to eligible households along with case management and other services to help families find and keep safe and permanent housing. The goal is to help families quickly get into a new home while building a foundation to maintain permanent housing. Families work with staff to establish a housing plan along with longer-range goals for self-sufficiency.

Aftercare—The *Aftercare* program is available to families as they exit Family Promise's emergency shelter and move into their new home. For nine months families work closely with Family Promise's case manager on self-determined goals related to long term independence. The goal is to help families maintain permanent housing and build assets to support self-sufficiency.

Staff

Family Promise staff includes an executive director, an assistant director/*Partners in Housing* manager, a Housing and Family Services program manager, a director of development, a Day Center staff person, a director of operations, a Sunday staff member and a van driver. An AmeriCorps member coordinates volunteers, furniture donations and the *Kids Care* program. A 17-person board of directors oversees Family Promise, along with a 4-member advisory board.

Partners

Family Promise is blessed to have sixteen host congregations who house families overnight on a regular basis. They are:

Calvin CRC	Mayflower Congregational
Cornerstone Church	Neland Avenue CRC
East Congregational UCC	Plymouth UCC
Fifth Reformed Church	Plymouth Heights CRC
First United Methodist Church	Princeton CRC
Genesis United Methodist Church	St. Andrew's Episcopal Church
Grace Episcopal Church	Southside Vineyard
Ivanrest CRC	Trinity Lutheran Church

An additional 22 area churches serve as support congregations that pitch in and help host congregations. Dozens of foundations, local businesses and community organizations are involved in volunteering, providing financial support and donating in-kind gifts to support the organization.

Funding

Family Promise of Grand Rapids is funded through the generous financial support of many in the community. Funding comes from businesses, congregations, foundations, United Way and individuals. Since 2002 an annual golf outing, *Changing the Course for Children*, has raised significant funds to support the shelter program. In 2013 Family Promise of Grand Rapids held its first *Dreams Dinner* celebration at which National Family Promise founder Karen Olson received a Lifetime Achievement Award. The following year the second *Dreams Dinner* attracted over 400 supporters.

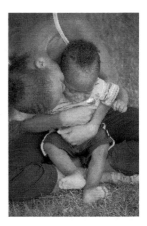

Monetary donations are always welcome, as are appliances, furniture, household goods, linens, nonperishable food items, landscape materials, tools and manufactured homes. In high demand are hygiene products, baby products, clothing, bus tickets, gas cards, gift cards to Walmart, Meijer and Family Dollar, medical and first aid supplies and household products.

Vision

The mission of Family Promise of Grand Rapids is to engage community and faith-based organizations to end homelessness, one family at a time. It pledges to:

- Help homeless families with children find permanent housing, and, through a continuum of supportive programs, help them achieve sustainable self-sufficiency.
- Be sensitive to and help families who are homeless due to situations (job loss) and/or are experiencing a life crisis (illness, divorce, domestic abuse), which has led to first-time, and for many, only-time, homelessness.
- Allow families to remain intact during a housing crisis so dads can stay with their families and boys over the age of 10 can remain with their siblings and parents. This lessens the negative impact on families and children. Separation adds additional stress and takes time away from the goals of securing permanent housing and employment.
- Maintain an 85% or greater rate of families served moving into permanent housing.
- Work with families to assure that 80% or more remain self-sufficient for one year or more.

Executive Director since 2009, Cheryl Schuch says, "The future of the children we serve is what drives our programs. Thousands of children have come through our doors, but each day we focus on each child and family—individually—to meet them where they are and make sure they have what they need to thrive. These children deserve the best we have and our community will be stronger because of the work we do today. They will grow into the leaders of tomorrow."

Mary Ann March
Founder

By the mid-1990s the Mission and Community Outreach group at East Congregational United Church of Christ in Grand Rapids had grown weary of writing checks to charities and donating canned goods to a local food pantry. They wanted something more. "We wanted to engage with the community while using the resource of our spacious building," says committee member Mary Ann March. "We wanted to do something hands-on; we wanted our outreach to have a human connection."

Happily, "East Church," as it is known, had recently engaged Brian Byrne as their new pastor. Brian said he knew just what they needed—the Interfaith Hospitality Network (IHN). He went on to explain that his former church had been a host site for IHN, a group of faith-based congregations that took turns providing emergency shelter for homeless families.

"We realized this was a perfect fit for our membership and the use of our building," says Mary Ann. "Brian was right—it was exactly what we were looking for."

According to Mary Ann, Brian was the catalyst. He sent letters to every pastor in town to explain the program and followed up with those who were interested. When he had commitments from eight churches, he set up an organizational meeting and invited IHN founder, Karen Olson, to speak. "Her story inspired us," says Mary Ann. "We realized that we could do what she had done."

There was still a lot of work to do before the IHN could become functional in Grand Rapids. A board of directors was seated, nonprofit status sought and granted, a part-time director, Kay Bylenga, was hired, and space for a Day Center was identified on the second floor of Burton Heights United Methodist Church.

As East Church's coordinator, Mary Ann put out the word to her congregation and soon had a bevy of volunteers. She chaired monthly meetings with the other host congregation coordinators so everyone could share their progress along the way. "The setup for East Church was relatively easy," says Mary Ann, "because the entire third floor of our church, which had formerly been Sunday School classrooms, was empty." Church members painted and set up the requisite five bedrooms and a lounge area with television and games and collected linens, furniture, toys and books. Mary Ann identified assistant coordinators to arrange for meals, play time, overnight hosts and supplies. With lots of energy and enthusiasm, Grand Rapids' Interfaith Hospitality Network was opened for business less than a year later, in July 1997.

Mary Ann sees the Interfaith Hospitality Network and Family Promise as an outreach program in which congregants of various ages and work schedules can participate. Between 50 and 75 volunteers are needed for a myriad of tasks each time a church hosts. "There's a role for everyone," Mary Ann says, "from cooking a meal, to playing with children, to moving the beds in and out.

"For the past decade," she continues, "St. Stephen's Catholic Church has been our Support Congregation, and they completely host two of the seven days on East Church's schedule." The hosts and hostesses from each congregation take pride in providing a welcoming and friendly atmosphere for their guests, just as they would in their own homes.

Through her commitment over the past 17 years, Mary Ann and the other legions of volunteers have learned much about the root causes of homelessness and the ramifications that make life so difficult for them. Mary Ann says, "Family Promise holds sensitivity training classes for all volunteers, whereby we become aware of issues the families face such as transportation challenges, the near impossibility of supporting a family with a minimum wage job and the lack of affordable housing in the area. We also take a look at ourselves and become more mindful of the ways we interact with the families."

Family Promise has changed Mary Ann's life. "I've met people I would otherwise never have met," she says. "I've seen firsthand how much the parents love their children and want what's best for them. I see how hard they struggle to provide for their children by taking buses in all kinds of weather and working third shifts at low-paying jobs. I know them and their struggles; they have faces and names, and that makes it very personal. I also love providing hospitality to the families; for just that one week, I can make an impact on the comfort and safety of 14 people who would otherwise be on the streets. I love that I'm part of the many people at Family Promise and in the community who seek to walk beside them."

Father Mike Fedewa
Host Congregation Pastor and Board Member

Father Mike Fedewa had been pastor of St. Andrew's Episcopal Church for about four years when he heard East Church's pastor Brian Byrne explain and promote the Interfaith Hospitality Network at a meeting of local clergy. "The program was just getting started," says Mike, "and St. Andrew's agreed to become the 13th host congregation. I thought that meant we'd have 13 weeks to  prepare, so I was mildly alarmed when we were assigned to be the third congregation on the schedule. But our church members jumped right in and pulled it off."

Quarterly, four co-coordinators at St. Andrew's rally between 45 and 60 volunteers to provide hospitality to the guests Family Promise sends for the week. Their Sunday School rooms are efficiently converted to guest bedrooms, meals are prepared and overnight assignments made. "This is the central community effort of our membership," says Mike. "Many volunteer because they like the 'people' aspect of the commitment, they can do more than donate money and they give of themselves. Some of our families bring their children to participate, too. I stay overnight at least one night each time St. Andrew's hosts."

Mike continues, "We've always had the sense that by God's grace we could make this work. From the very beginning members had a sense of vitality and energy that gave us confidence in other ministries we took on as well."

Acting as a host congregation has opened members' eyes to the realities faced by many families—all sorts of crises, including unemployment, addictions, medical issues and financial burdens. "Every family without a home has their own unique story," says Mike. "There's not just one story of the path to homelessness. Despite all the setbacks they deal with, I am amazed by the resourcefulness guest families employ to make things work. I look at the ease which with I start my day, with coffee and a hot shower, things I take for granted. Then I look at the families we host. It takes an incredible amount of energy, creativity and resourcefulness for them just to start the day and get the kids to school. It's astounding to me."

Kathy Griffes is Church Administrator at St. Andrew's, which is located on Three Mile Road NE, and she has also been involved with Family Promise since its inception in Grand Rapids. "I've spent many nights in the chapel, listening, praying and crying with some of our guests," says Kathy.

"You really connect with people and grow to love the families. I remember so many men and women and their stories. Then the week comes to an end and you cry to lose them."

Kathy emphasizes that the role she and other volunteers at St. Andrew's play is that of listener, not fixer. That's Family Promise's job. "It's a ministry of presence," she says. "You just need to be there with an open heart and an open mind. To 'be' and to follow their cues. God is in, around and through all of this, and He works wonders."

In 2012, Mike was asked to become a Family Promise board member, an experience that has given him a broader perspective of the complexities of homelessness. He is struck by the growth of Interfaith Hospitality Network into all that Family Promise offers today. "It's no longer just about shelter," says Mike, "it's about so much more, such as mentoring programs, follow up, and behind-the-scenes work. The organization seeks to address the needs of families before they get into crisis situations and lose their homes. I believe Family Promise is the best homeless prevention and crisis program in the community."

Calvin College StreetFest students showed hospitality by cooking "move-in meals" for Family Promise families who were blessed with new homes.

Mike has seen ripple effects from St. Andrew's involvement as a host congregation. "Churches in our area know we're involved," he says. "One of my family members belongs to another church, and her congregation is now involved with IHN and Family Promise. Ripples abound."

He concludes, "Hospitality is a prime tenet of the Christian faith. The weeks we have guests stay with us are the holiest of the year. They are the face of Christ."

Tabetha
IHN and PIH Participant

Several years ago, Tabetha moved to Grand Rapids with a female friend. Both women were single mothers with children; Tabetha had two young boys, Vick, Jr. and Treyton, and her friend had three children. The pair struggled to find affordable housing and sought help at the Salvation Army, which, in turn, referred the women to Family Promise. Thus began Tabetha's relationship with the nonprofit that has been instrumental in changing her life.

"The people at Family Promise helped us find a home to rent," says Tabetha, now 26. "It had four bedrooms, two baths and a fenced-in yard. It was wonderful." Tabetha and her friend received subsidy funding from another agency and, over a period of six months, paid a little more of the actual cost each month until they were able to cover the full payments themselves.

Tabetha took advantage of Family Promise's resources to conduct job searches on their computers, get references, schedule interviews and use bus passes for transportation. She soon found work as a server at a local restaurant, a job she enjoyed.

Some months later Tabetha and her friend parted ways, and Tabetha, facing homelessness again, sought a house of her own. She lived with her mother up north for several months while working with Barbara Zylstra, Family Promise's Assistant Director and Administrator of the Partners in Housing (PIH) program. "Barbara taught me on the budgeting process," says Tabetha, "and we explored my ability to own a home through the PIH program. Through monthly budget meetings and financial counseling, Barbara helped me move into a manufactured home in Wyoming owned by Family Promise."

Treyton, Tabetha's younger son, was only six months old when she first came to Family Promise, and the organization provided diapers, formula, baby clothes and other supplies so she could save every possible dollar for her goal of home ownership. "That made it really helpful to save up and get to where I am now," says Tabetha.

Family Promise worked closely with Tabetha to ensure she would stay on track financially and "not backslide," as Tabetha says. "They give me so much support. Whenever I need direction or help in any area, I call Family Promise. They gave me their cell phone numbers and email addresses and encouraged me to contact them at any time. I know they're always there for me."

Before moving into the manufactured home in January 2013, Family Promise volunteers rehabbed the structure. Tabetha continued under case management for six months, paying her rent and utilities on time and demonstrating proper upkeep inside and out. After staying within the guidelines for six months, Tabetha became a homeowner. Since then, she remains in communication with Family Promise twice a month. "The follow-up is very helpful," says Tabetha.

"I'm so proud of Tabetha," says PIH Director Barbara Zylstra. "She's tenacious about her goals to improve her life and displays real drive. Throughout the process she stayed in touch with us, despite personal ups and downs, car troubles and day care issues. Tabetha rises above her problems in an amazing way. She has a beautiful, radiant smile that reveals her inner light. She went from homelessness to homeownership."

Recently Tabetha found a new job at a local electronics company with regular hours and a flexible schedule, which comes in handy because of the needs of her boys, now ages six and three. In addition, she works a few shifts at the restaurant each month to increase her income.

Tabetha's family has grown with a significant other and his child, so she's exploring the possibility of buying a bigger home. She's also thinking about going back to school within the next year to further her nursing education.

"Family Promise helped me gain a better outlook on life," says Tabetha. "Before, I kind of sat back and hoped my goals would happen some day. There were always setbacks and struggles. With Family Promise I think, 'Wow! I can do this.' They are willing to help you better yourself. They push you to reach your goals. I would definitely recommend Family Promise to others and tell them not to be afraid to turn to someone for help if they need it.

"There would be a whole lot of people out there struggling," Tabetha continues, "if it weren't for Family Promise. In the weeks and months I received mentoring and counseling, they were helping many other people. They make time for each individual, each family. They put a lot of time and effort into what they do, and I am so grateful to them."

Juanita Sanchez and LaDale Nelson
Family

For Juanita Sanchez and her family, 2012 was a horrible year. A downward spiral began when, pregnant with her fourth child, Juanita was diagnosed with breast cancer. Unable to retain her job in a retail store due to chemotherapy and two operations, she couldn't contribute to the family income. Her husband LaDale Nelson wasn't able to pay the bills from his employment at a local grocery store, then a restaurant. Consequently, the Sanchez family lost the home they rented and began to live in their older-model van. They had to leave all their furniture and household goods behind, along with most of their clothing, because there was no place to store them. Then LaDale lost his job. Now they were two adults, three teenaged children and a new baby, living in a van. Then the van broke down. On top of everything else, the baby, Alianna, was born with a mild case of Down syndrome. "We had so much bad luck," says Juanita.

Ever resourceful, she dialed "2-1-1," the telephone number to connect with human services, and was referred to The Salvation Army, who referred Juanita to Family Promise. "I made an appointment," she says, "and the first thing they did was give us emergency shelter through the Interfaith Hospitality Network (IHN). We lived in the various host congregations for a little over a month."

In the meantime, Juanita and LaDale availed themselves of the services provided by Family Promise's Day Center. "Our children, ages 14, 15, and 17, went to school every day while LaDale and I used the expertise of the Family Promise staff and their resources to look for jobs and housing. It was stressful not having a home, especially with a newborn and undergoing radiation for my breast cancer, but it was so much better than living on the streets."

Juanita says that Family Promise supplied them with all the tools for successful house and job hunting and the couple did the legwork. She enrolled for Medicaid online. The staff and volunteers were also there for the family emotionally. "Sometimes I just wanted to cry," says Juanita. "I felt hopeless. They cheered me up and told me we'd get through this crisis. You get into moods where it's overwhelming—you want to give up, but I never did because the people at Family Promise were behind me, supporting me."

Juanita found a home and volunteers from host congregations provided the family with clothing, linens and furniture for their new home. Both LaDale and Juanita found new jobs. "The whole experience was a blessing in a way, because, with Family Promise's help, we ended up in a better situation than we had previously," says Juanita.

Their two-year-old daughter is doing well. "She's pretty smart," says Juanita. "I was worried about having my surgeries while she was developing in the womb, but she is healthy and happy." Their two oldest sons, now 23

164

and 18, moved out of the family home and are doing well with jobs and housing on their own. Their teenage daughter Sabrina is able to watch little Alianna when Juanita is at work. Blessedly, Juanita is cancer-free.

Juanita stays in touch with some of the other families she met through Family Promise and checks in with the agency weekly. She has also referred others she knows in crisis situations to Family Promise for help. "It's an excellent program," she says. "Words cannot describe how I feel about what they do to help people."

She continues, "I never thought I would be homeless. I had a job and paid my bills. Then, all of a sudden, everything went wrong. If it wasn't for Family Promise, I don't know what would have happened to my family. We'd be living in our van or out on the streets. We got back on our feet because of Family Promise."

Their commitment has inspired Juanita to give back to the agency that helped her so much. She is currently volunteering as an inspirational speaker, telling her story to groups in the hope of raising awareness and support for Family Promise. "I'm excited to help them in any way I can," says Juanita.

Julie
Guest

Julie, a single mother of two, runs a molding machine at a local plastics company for $13 an hour. Her boyfriend, and the father of her younger son, lives with them and works a seasonal job. Their combined incomes are just enough to pay the rent, utilities and other expenses such as trash removal and yard maintenance. Julie drives an older model Chevrolet Cobalt. They eat noodles, hot dogs and peanut butter and jelly sandwiches for dinner.

"I wish I could afford to buy my sons better food, like fruits and vegetables," says Julie, age 33, "but I'm on a tight budget. I can't buy them the extras that they would enjoy."

Julie defines the term "working poor."

Born in Nunica, Michigan, Julie and her son Dominic moved to New Orleans in 2008, where her father lives. When Julie became the victim of domestic abuse, she fled back to Michigan. Her mother, still living in Nunica, took Julie and Dominic in. Julie found a job in Grand Rapids and also began taking Criminal Justice classes at ITT Technical Institute. "The drive into Grand Rapids was taking too much time and gas money, so Dominic and I moved in with a friend in the city," says Julie. Splitting the rent worked for a while, but after a falling out, Julie and Dominic left the apartment with nowhere to go. They stayed in her car and in motel rooms, but that soon got to be expensive.

Julie met her boyfriend Chuck and the two had a baby boy, Zion, in 2011. Julie transferred to Grand Rapids Community College (GRCC) to pursue her dream of getting her Associates degree and becoming a juvenile probation officer while holding down a full-time job.

Julie came to Family Promise in 2012 and was given shelter through the *Interfaith Hospitality Network*. "They were a big help," says Julie. "I was working second shift, so I woke up at the church, drove to the Day Center, did my research on housing leads, took the kids to a sitter, went to work, picked the kids up, and got back to the church after everyone else had arrived. The church volunteers always kept dinner warm for us."

There was an eviction on Julie's record, so that made it more difficult to find a place to live. After a month she finally found a house where the landlord would work with her, and her mother helped out with some money to get started. "We lived in that home for a year and a half," says Julie, "but the conditions were awful, with little insulation, broken windows, rodents and cockroaches. Some months our gas bill was $600 because of the poor insulation. I ended up vacating with another eviction on my record."

Facing eviction and homelessness again, Julie again called Family Promise and Lisa Cruden, Housing and Family Services Program Manager, helped Julie find temporary housing in partnership with another agency.

The family was there for a few months when Julie hurt her back and was forced to have hernia, then back, surgery. She had no choice but to drop out of GRCC. Unable to take care of herself and the kids, Chuck moved in as caretaker. As Julie recuperated, Family Promise helped her continue her search for permanent housing. The agency came through for Julie again when Debbie, a volunteer with connections to real estate and landlords, found a duplex for rent. Julie, Chuck and the boys were able to move into the house where they've been for the past few months. "It's in a good neighborhood and we feel safe and independent," says Julie. "I have my family back together."

Family Promise is a place of refuge, according to Julie. "Even though I'm out on my own now, Family Promise still helps me when I need food, pull-up diapers for Zion or help with my budgeting. They provided new work shoes when mine wore out. They also gave Dominic a backpack filled with school supplies in late August. Those things mean a lot to me."

Whenever Julie feels hopeless, discouraged, or overwhelmed, she calls Lisa at Family Promise. "She listens and helps keep my spirits up," says Julie.

Despite all the challenges in her life, Julie tries to keep a positive attitude. "My main goal is simply to live in my house with my family; live my life day-to-day and be happy."

About the Authors

A sixth-generation Grand Rapidian, **Deb Moore** owns *The Stories of Your Life*, a service that helps individuals, families, businesses and churches preserve and record their histories. As a personal historian, Deb has helped more than 50 people write their life stories since 2003 and preserve them as books. She also conducted interviews for the "SOUL of Philanthropy" project to record the reflections of top local philanthropists for the documentary film that aired on public television, *The Gift of All—A Community of Givers*. Deb has made numerous presentations on memoir-writing at Calvin College's Youth Writers' Festival, Aquinas College's OLLI Program, Calvin College's CALL Program, local schools, libraries, assisted living facilities and senior clubs. Visit Deb's website at www.TheStoriesOfYourLife.com.

Betty Epperly is the daughter of Dutch immigrants who settled on a farm in West Michigan. Despite many obstacles and through much sacrifice, they ensured that their five children would have the benefit of a college education. People who have overcome challenges throughout history inspired Betty to start *Crooked Tree Stories*, a service in which she assists people in writing their memoirs and life stories. She has mentored young people in publishing their short stories and novels. As an instructor at Forest Hills Community Center, Betty has helped people publish their nonfiction and fiction works. This year she will teach the *Legacy Project*, which will enable seniors to preserve their memories and experiences for generations to come. Betty's website is www.crookedtreestories.com.

Deb and Betty are members of the *Association of Personal Historians*, a worldwide organization of 650+ members whose purpose is to advance the profession of assisting individuals, organizations and communities to preserve their histories, life stories and memories.